RIGHT HAND BLUE

Vicki Gage

Art by: Dan Gagen

This book is dedicated to

My parents Bob and Fran

Kitt Gibson

And

Tim Wagner

I want to say hey to all of my men Kris, Kyle, Jacob, Austin and Levi. Hello to my girls Alexx, Danni, Emily and Andrea.

The art in this book are pieces of a puzzle for you to put together to create a copy of an original painting by Dan Gagen.

Lori, I love you for all of the red marks. My punctuation sucks!

Ken and Sue, I love you both to the moon and back.

Hassie and Kathy, I love going back in time with you.

"T", your blessing means the world to me.

My family at work. We may be the island of misfit toys but when we all come together….look out.

Thank you all very much for being part of this incredible trip!!

Thank you for buying my book…enjoy the ride.

Love you all…peace out.

Until next time…

Chapter One

Air whipping through my hair on the back of a bike. Is there any place in the world better to let my thoughts run wild? I have my legs wrapped around my man Lin and everything in life is temporarily put on hold. I never realized going through the normal everyday (or should I say every year) life with kids how the phrase "a fork in the road" really carries meaning until they don't need me anymore.

Life for the last 21 years has been driven by the force of what will make everyone else happy. It is a hard concept when you finally get to say to yourself "what do I want? " How pathetic is it when all you can say is, I don't have a fucking clue what I want or how to do it. The last few years have not been easy but I wouldn't trade them for anything. The only thing I would change is for Tim to be here to watch his boys on their journey, as they grow into men. Being both mother and father has had many unpredictable valleys and peaks. I really lucked out hooking up with Lin. Funny story that one, neither of us were looking for love. We found it wanting to come out of hiding in each other. Thank you, Ray! You little match maker you. Between Lin's two and my two, the kids have kept us busy trying to guide them through life decisions and choices.

Thomas, at 26, is the oldest. He is married to Poppy, an awesome English girl he met during his stint with the United States Air Force. They are making their way as every young couple starting out does. Allen is 22, in a relationship with Nicki and they are thinking about buying a house. Nichole is 21 and has her own place. Living the dream and having fun along the way. Henry the baby at 18, is the last to leave the nest. Baseball has been very good to him and he has a full scholarship to learn. He will start his adventure playing a game he loves. We will be moving him to college in a few months. All four kids are taking a very different trip.

I know what Lin is thinking about. We have an opportunity to travel the world, just the two of us. He has been offered a job that pays enough money for me to quit work and start my own new unchartered adventure. I am not very good with the unpredictable. Case in point: I have lived in the same small county in Indiana for 99.9% of my life. I am not complaining. I love my small town where everyone knows everyone and everyone knows everyone else's business. It has been a great place to raise kids. Now we are thinking about selling our home and buying a travel trailer to move around the planet. Going wherever the work takes us. I haven't even told Michael and Eric (my bosses) that I am leaving them yet. Don't get me wrong, I absolutely love my job on most days but there is a little voice inside me that says I deserve to be me and open a new chapter in my life with Lin.

"Molly! Hey Molly! Let's stop for a smoke."

I snap back to reality. I look around and notice we are out in the middle of BFE. Go to the second silo and turn left. Green fields of corn as far as the eye can see. An abundance of orange tiger lilies around the edges. This is what riding is all about. Finding a spot where the only other mammal around are the two cats hunting in the ditch across the dirt road. There is more oxygen here than one body can suck in.

I am right. I can tell as we get off the bike that Lin has been thinking about the new job offer. He wastes no time opening his mouth to let his thoughts fall out.

"I say we do it Mol. I mean think about it. We can roll with it like we are two young kids starting a new adventure. The only difference is we will have enough money to do it large and right…our way. I have been making a mental list of the pros and cons. The biggest "con" is the work it will take to make this happen."

Lin sure can plead a case when it is something he really wants. In my black and white world I have to say to him "I agree with you Lin, but I am telling you straight up, I don't do well with unknowns. We can't make an educated decision until we have all of the facts."

He gets a sparkle in his eye and says "All the better baby. We will figure it out together by the seat of our pants. No one to answer to but us. I love what I do, and it is not really work for me. This job offer couldn't have come at a better time. You can write that book you always talk about. Henry is almost done with High

School. His map is planned for the next four years. The other kids have started their journey, so why can't we? Let's ride for a few more miles and stop at this little antique shop called "Time". I passed it on my way home from the last job. You chew on what I just said for awhile. I know you will let me know when you are ready to spit it out."

The shop is really like something you would see in the 1920's. Steps leading down to a basement shop with wrought iron rails out front. This is not even the best part. As you walk through the doorway of beads, you get a whiff of strawberry incense burning. Now that brings back memories I will tell you about later (tehehe). I can honestly say this is not your normal antique place. There doesn't seem to be much inventory. Everything is very clean but, I feel a going out of business sale in the near future. What is here is high class stuff. Beautiful treasure boxes, exquisite scarves, a wall of jewelry cases. This place has what a true picker would call lots of expensive "smalls".

Lin seems to be a little disappointed since there are no old motorcycles taking up space, although he has found some old magazines full of bike pictures and detailed drawings. He has always been a sucker for old ads that have bikes with pin-up girls. I have decided to see if they have any charms to add to my bracelet. I think I have space for one more charm, but I don't see anything that strikes my fancy. Lots of costume jewelry and gold chains; a couple pretty cameo lockets, but I don't like wearing necklaces. Before I can walk away from the glass displays I feel a cold hand on mine. There looking at me is a man who appears to be about 150 years old.

"Let me see dat" pointing at my wrist?

I look around at Lin, deep into his magazine, he has no idea this man is giving me the heebie jeebies. I reluctantly put my other hand on the counter.

I was given the bracelet as a high school graduation present, and over the years I have added charms that remind me of the special places in my life. He points at a few of the charms and I tell him brief descriptions of my life of babies, watching my boys grow up, and the Beatles charm I saved up for. The whole time I am talking, the old man just smiles and nods his head as if he knows because he has been there.ABruptly, he turns and walks through a curtain behind the counter. Mind you, he doesn't say a word no "excuse me", "hang on I will be right back" or "kiss my ass and get out of my shop." Before I can get Lins attention and get the hell out of Dodge, the little old man is walking back towards me holding his own charm bracelet. Just by looking at it, I can tell that some of these beautiful charms are very, very old. As he hands it to me he utters "My Momma."

Each charm is special and unique. I notice there is a space where a charm has been taken off. It makes me wonder how beautiful the missing charm must be. I ask him if any of the charms are for sale. Have you ever had that feeling when you ask someone a question and they just stand there and stare into your soul? He doesn't say a word but turns around to go through the same curtain to the back room. Now I am curious. What is he doing? Will he come back, since I am still holding his bracelet? I see him backing up towards me, parting the curtains. He must be speaking to someone in the other room because I swear I hear him say "I am tired." Now he is walking towards me, and I see he is carrying a small ornate box. He takes back his ring of charms and hands me the box. I wonder if this is the missing piece to his bracelet, why did he take it off and how much is this going to cost me? As I am about to lift the clasp and open the box the old man covers my hand with his and gives me a look like he has something to say that I better listen to. You know the one your father gives you when you are in trouble. He mutters four words "Be learning seeing eyes." He points to his head, then he puts his pointer finger in front of his lips and whispers "shhhh".

Silently I watch him walk back through the curtain and as I go to open the box again Lin gives me one of his sweet pinches on the ass. This means "let's hit the road, nothing for me here." Before I can even turn around to tell him what just happened, all of the lights go out. I hear a door open behind the counter across from me. No bumping into objects sounds. That is what you would expect to hear in this pitch black room. Damn baby, pay your light bill. Then, all of a sudden, the bright sun shines in through the front door. There, holding the door open for us to leave is a small boy. He also gives me the "Shhh" sign and says "take the box and go". Is it just me or would you be saying to yourself "What the fuck just happened?" Maybe I should quit smoking pot, because this shit doesn't happen to me. Is someone going to walk out and say "Smile you're on Candid Camera?" In my stupor, unable to vocalize, Lin grabs my hand and out the door we go.

As we sit by the bike to have one last smoke, I open the box. The charm is about the size of a sugar cube. It is green jade, carved with little smooth intertwining vines and peephole windows. On the top, there is a little gold fastener for attaching it to a bracelet. As I hold it up in the sunshine I see the twinkle of a diamond suspended inside the cube. This is unlike any charm I have ever seen. I guarantee it's the oldest one I have ever seen. It must be worth a fortune! Lin's only comment is "Maybe you remind him of someone from his past or he's just being nice to a beautiful woman. You can mail him a thank you note when we get home". He is ready to head down the road, so we assume our positions. As we pull away, I turn around to look at the shop. I see the old man standing on the curb. He looks so lonely and old. He has his hand over his mouth and a very lost look in his eyes.

The next seventy miles go past me in what seems to be a matter of minutes. Just the screams from my bladder and the urge for a smoke brings me out of my deep thoughts. I cannot, for the life of me, figure out why I was given such a beautiful gift. The whole thing is too weird and amazing to rationalize. I need to stop thinking about it for now. Every direction my thoughts take leads to wait and see what shakes out. I need to come back to the here and now. Lin and I are two great minds that think alike. My man is reading my vibes and pulling into a hotel. Yes! My kingdom for a nice long bath, a beer, and a fatty.

The hotel isn't much, but it does have a really cool claw foot bathtub. After Lin and I get something to eat we plan to get a six pack and soak in the tub. That sounds like a very relaxing evening to me. Unfortunately, Lin doesn't make it that far. A man with a full belly, plus a long day on a bike equals, falling asleep with your boots on, as they say. Oh well, this means I get to use the "girlie smelling" bath oil. Bathtub here I come! Three beers in the ice bucket? Check. Smokes? Check. Candles burning? Check. I think I have everything I want. I even have the box holding my new charm so I can put this new story on my wrist. The tub has one of those trays that will stretch across the top, so doing this as I soak won't be a problem.

Show me a mother who doesn't enjoy her "alone time" and I will kiss your ass. Laying back in a warm bath with a slight buzz, knowing the day has been good. That everyone you love is alright, and the only requirement right now is to just relax, is priceless. All of that rolled into one, is hard to get but much appreciated. I lay back, listen to the crickets outside the open window, take a deep breath and unplug. I melt into the peaceful song of the night critters.

Time to get back to reality. Besides I am starting to look like a prune and the beer is all gone. It was nice while it lasted, but the water is getting cold. It doesn't help that my calming night song has been interrupted by a barking, pissed off dog.

I pick up my bracelet. The new addition is perfect. Here is my kitten, for my sister Kitt. I miss her cute, sweet face every day. Here is the charm I had made from my wedding ring. I know Kitt and Tim have found each other. Just the thought of that reunion brings a warm smile and a giggle, even if I am standing in a bathroom all by myself. Here is my new charm. That one is a

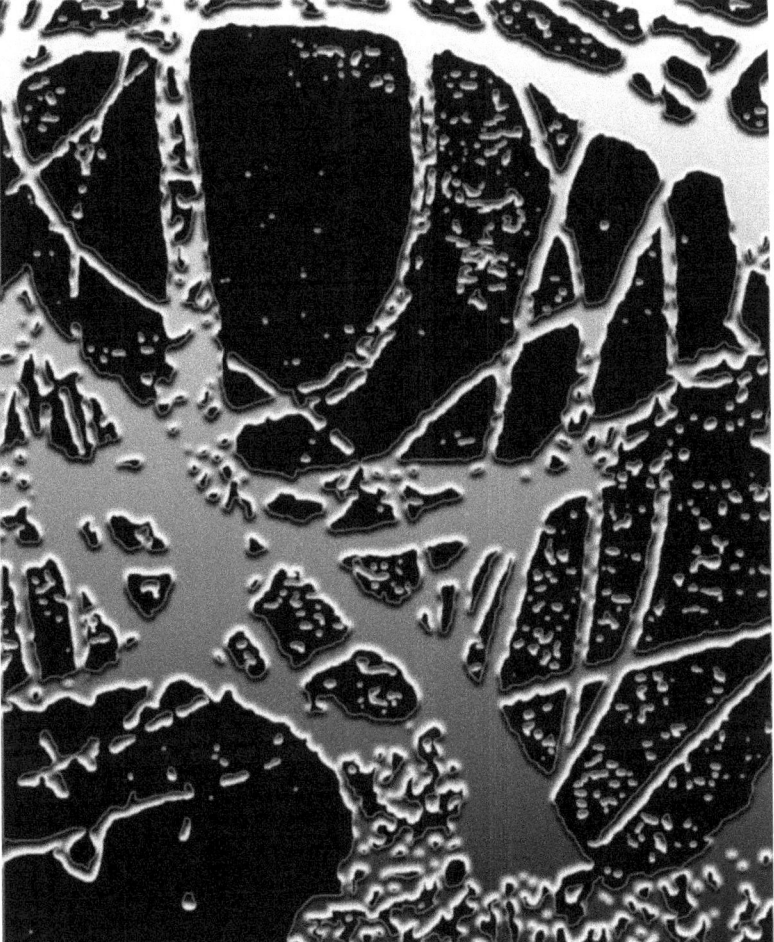

Chapter Two

Bizarre story. Where did the bath tub go? It was close enough for me to sit on a minute ago. One sweep of my hand tells me, nope nothing there. Why is it so dark? Where are the candles that were burning? This is not your normal "oh damn the lights went out" moment. I am not counting on electricity this time. Did I fall and bump my head? Great! If I don't wake up, I won't be found until Lin has to take a piss in the morning. Won't he be surprised? Am I dreaming? Have I died or am I lying passed out in the middle of the bathroom floor? I don't think I have lost my mind. I have always been told, crazy people don't know they're crazy. Freaking out isn't a want, or an option. That doesn't mean I am not thinking WTF. Keep it to a mild roar here Molly. Freak out later.

It is so quiet in here. Where did the crickets and the barking dog go? If a mouse walked across the floor right now, I think I would hear it. Oddly enough, it is not a creepy scary quiet but calm, soothing and peaceful. Damn, I hope I remember this because I think I might, in some strange way enjoy the ride.

Wait a minute I have been here. I smell strawberry incense. A little more light would be wonderful. No pockets in the towel I'm wearing means no lighter. Shit! If I am where my nose thinks I am (what are the odds of that) the window should be over there. With my arms out in front of me, I take tiny steps. This could hurt. Alright jewelry case…got it…side step to the right. The counter ends by the wall with the door and the only window. I turn the corner and side step right. Yep, here are the curtains. They are like the thick, heavy curtains you see in a theater or on a stage. They remind me of the heavy duty curtains that hung on the stage in Cromwell Elementary. Memory flash! The band director who wore band-aids behind his ears and sucked on lifesavers all the time.

Isn't it amazing what a little light can bring onto a subject? My nose was right…I am in "Time".

Glancing around, the shop hasn't changed. I still don't see anything that interests me. Why am I here or am I? I bump my head and this is where I land? That's pathetic, Molly. I think about the little old man and his fascination with the back room. I wonder what wonderful things could be on the other side of that curtain. There is only one way to find out. Come on feet move!   The window offers little light since the only source is from one lamp on the sidewalk outside. Here we go Molly, shuffle left until you find the walk through opening. Walk straight through the curtain doorway.

Logic tells me that most light switches are beside any given doorway. Voila....Houston we have light!

The room is about the size of a two car garage. The walls are lined with huge bookcases. Like those you would find in a library. There is a square wooden table in the center of the room. That is all there is. No chairs. No desks. Nothing on any of the shelves. They look as if they have been empty for a long time. There are no tell tale signs of anything ever being kept here, just a thick blanket of dust and cobwebs. It is almost as though someone moved out years ago. No one builds this kind of shelving to sit empty, how odd and sad. On the table there is a small safety deposit box and a key.

If curiosity killed the cat then I am in big trouble and taking my last breath. Hell, for all I know I am already dead on the bathroom floor! The powers that be must be busy or they have forgotten about me. The key fits the deposit box, one mystery solved. What is the point of having a safety box if you leave it out in the open with the fucking key? It is almost like they have been discarded as junk. The inside of the box is lined in red crushed velvet with a cut out that holds a small purple velvet box. I open the smaller box. It is also lined but it has seen better days. There is an indentation that looks like a nest to hold a perfect little square. It appears it held one for many years. The cushion is worn, faded and has a small tear in it. Could this be the old home to my new charm?

Why would he put the charm into a different box just to give it to me? Maybe he was just being nice. This little velvet box is tattered, not very pretty and smells musty. This charm must be worth a King's ransom. Why else would you keep it under lock and key? Note to self: get an appraisal for insurance purposes. Just for shits and giggles, I want to know if this box once belonged to my charm. As long as no one can get hurt, why leave a theory or experiment untested? To remove the charm I have to pinch the

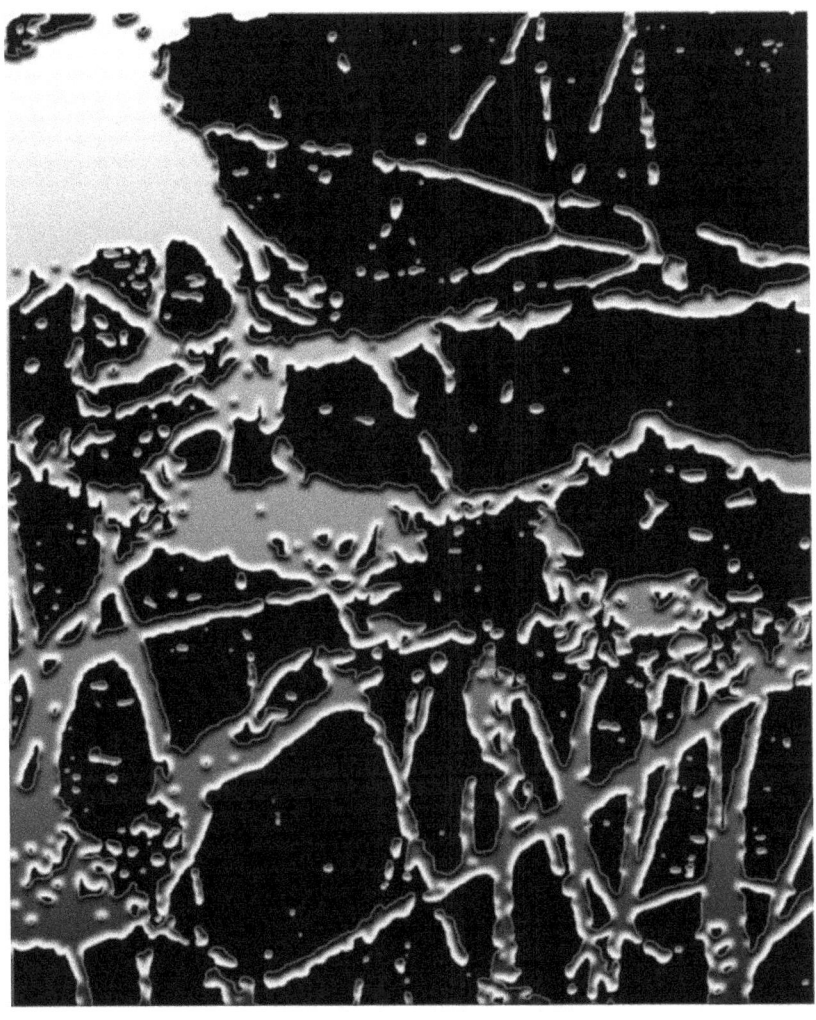

Chapter Three

Clasp. Holy Shit Batman!! What is it with me and the lights going out? Now I smell the strawberry incense being taken over by vanilla. Once my eyes adjust, I realize I am standing in the hotel bathroom again, facing the tub, still full of water but draining out. The candles are still burning. Lin is snoring in the next room. I am holding the jade charm in my hand. Didn't I just attach this to my bracelet? How did it come off?

Man, I think I need to go to bed. Did I really just fall asleep standing up? The dream I just had felt so real. The sights, the smells, the way the curtains felt when I rubbed them. I can still taste a hint of the strawberry smell. Did I just have an out of body experience? I'm not saying it can't happen but why not just float up and check out my own back side to see if my ass is getting big or worse flat? Why go back to Time? This shit is making my head spin, standing in the middle of this bathroom is getting me nowhere. I am going to crawl into bed, sleep on it, and see what rational thought the morning may bring. In my usual fashion I am asleep in a matter of seconds.

If you have ever had a dream that you can't seem to shake then you know where my mind is. I have no idea if I dreamed after I got into bed, but the one I had in the bathroom won't let go of my mind. Lin wakes me up with the chickens, ready to have coffee and breakfast, so we can get back on the road towards home. He is all bright eyed and bushy tailed. I feel like I am just going through the motions. What I really want right now is to be on the back of the bike where I can try to sort out this dream that keeps haunting me. I love these "no-purpose" road trips we make. It is a great way to clean out mental cob webs. Time to get out the broom.

After going through a hundred and fifty miles of thoughts. I have come to a conclusion. There are only two parts I can't explain how "it" happened. First, why did I wake up facing the tub? I specifically remember stepping out to dry off. I was facing the opposite wall, wrapping the towel around myself, looking at my new charm and thinking about the antique shop. Second, how did the charm come off of the bracelet? I remember in my dream pinching the clasp to take off the charm. I remember wanting to see if it fit in the little purple velvet box. I can still see the desolate back room, the safety deposit box on the table with the key right beside it. I remember thinking what a stupid way to guard your treasures and how sad it was that all of the shelves were empty. I have never been one to sleep walk or act out my dreams. Truth be told, once I am asleep I don't move at all until morning. I have never fallen asleep standing up.

This whole thing doesn't make any sense. It would probably be a good idea to start a journal and write this shit down. I need to get it out of my head and on paper. I just can't get past how real my dream felt, smelled, sounded and looked. If I tried to explain this to Lin, he would laugh at me and ask what I ate before I fell asleep.

As soon as we get home life goes back into its predictable timeline. Going to work every day, keeping a house, doing laundry, cooking, washing dishes. You know the ho-hum drill. I love my life and everything that comes with it, but it is easy to fall into a day in day out predictable pattern.

Henry is all but packed for his move. He has everything he needs to start college. He has always been my planner. You don't find him behind the eight ball very often. Now he is just enjoying the life of a teenager working part time, his senior year, baseball and hanging out with his friends.

Sunday mornings are the best for slow starts with Lin. Relaxed having our morning coffee, we enjoy the quiet time together doing whatever we choose to do. Brunch is over, dishes are done, and there is a roast cooking in the crock pot for dinner. Life is good and I am off the clock for awhile.

Lin decides to hang out in the garage to work on the 1952 Harley he has been restoring. This is not a project we can do together; a wrench head I am not. I am going to start that journal.

Because I am an insatiable reader, we put a couch in the garage so we can at least be in the same room while we do our own thing. It has been a week since my dream, but it feels like yesterday. Putting it to paper is not a problem and takes me no time at all. I have decided I fell asleep, but the experience is still worthy of writing down.

Next, I open the book I picked up recently. I have always been a history buff. I tend to pick a subject and just read the "shit out of it". I try to avoid the internet because it is usually full of crap anyway. Give me a good thick book any day! The book I have selected is a much loved and studied subject but this is an old book I have never read. It is about The Beatles. Ask me anything you want to know about the Fab Four and if it is published, I know it. I even had a question about the Beatles read on MTV once. There is my one minute of fame. I'm still waiting on the remaining fourteen.

As I do with every book I read, I flip to the pictures and check them out before I start reading. It helps me form a mental picture when the subject comes up in the book.

A couple of hours roll by. I have heard Lin cuss only once. If staring down a problem while deep in thought could solve the troubles of the world, my Lin would be the man for the job. We would all be shitting in high cotton. He is not a man who takes projects lightly nor is he one to attack them half assed. In our house we call it "whole-assed". I love watching my man work. It's a good day. The front fender is going on.

By now I have read past the childhoods of John, George and Paul, their trip to Hamburg Germany, and Stuart Sutcliffe. At this point they have come back home to unleash what they have learned on the crowd at the Cavern Club. I haven't learned anything new, but it doesn't hurt to refresh my mental files every once in awhile. Can you imagine what it was like to be part of that scene? There are so many points in rock history that would blow me away to see! Jimi setting his guitar on fire: Janis at the Monterey Pop Festival, the ultimate would be Woodstock.

I flip to the picture of an empty Cavern Club. I try to imagine being there, in that old wine cellar with no windows, no movement of air, and sweat

Chapter Four

Dripping down the walls. I look around, but there is not another living soul in the place. It isn't dark. I can hear muffled voices. It definitely isn't Lin talking, unless he has picked up a Liverpool "scouse" accent. The last time I had this sensation I was holding the charm and thinking about the antique shop. Now I am no longer sitting on the couch in our garage, but standing in a room that looks like the Cavern Club. I think back and wonder. Was I not paying attention, playing with my bracelet while I was looking at the pictures in the book?

The room is unbelievably hot and smells like a cross between a boy's locker room and a dirty bathroom with a dash of old cigarette smoke on the side. It isn't very wide but it is deep with tunnels shooting off of the room I am in. Large brick archways form the openings to each tunnel. There are a few folding chairs scattered around, but most of the floor space has been left open. There are three guitars, a small drum kit, a couple of amps, and microphones on the stage, which I am facing. The wall behind the stage is made out of large odd shaped flat stones. Each one painted a different color. It reminds me of the Partridge Family bus. There are words written on the stones. The only names I can read from where I stand are "The Beatles" and "Rory Storm and the Hurricanes". I have to get a closer look.

Oh Shit! One guitar is strung upside down for a left handed person. No way! Are you fucking kidding me? Is this, could this possibly be Paul's guitar? Now I know what those screaming girls on Ed Sullivan felt like because I can hardly contain myself. I want to touch and smell everything! I pick up a drum stick lying on the stage. Does this belong to Pete Best or Ringo? Did I just miss them, or are they still here? Oh yeah, Molly, what would you say if they did come walking in from another room? They would notice that something is odd. I mean really, you are wearing cut off jean shorts and a t-shirt that says Kid Rock "American Badass."

My ears perk up. Voices are heading this way. OMG! I have to hide or try to come up with a good reason why this chick, who is dressed funny, is standing on the stage touching all of the equipment. I make a mad dash for one of the dark tunnels.

If I get close to the floor and peek out maybe they won't notice me. This makes sense because the lights aren't that bright in here. Sure enough two guys come around the corner carrying brooms and trash cans. They are talking about the show from earlier tonight.

"Fred, whad ya think of that teddy boy Lennon?" asks the older-looking man.

Fred says "I had a class wif him in school. He is an alright bloke, even if he is a bit of a smart arse. Wicked tongue that one. Why do you ask"?

"I knew his mum before she died. She was an odd bird, but she always seemed to have on a smile. Sad story that one. Fred, you take the tunnels on the left and I will go this way. We'll meet in the middle. Let's get this done so I can go home to me misses. Leave the stage be. The boys'll be back for their gear after Mona feeds'em."

"Ok Edward, get on wif it then" replies Fred.

Oh shit oh double shit! Here comes Fred. Think Molly, think. What happened last time? I was taking off my charm to see if it fit in the little box. It was in my hand when I woke up in the bathroom. No time! Fred is about ten steps from finding me. I pop up off my belly into the dark, and fumble with the cube charm, trying to feel the clasp. Got it! Can it really be this

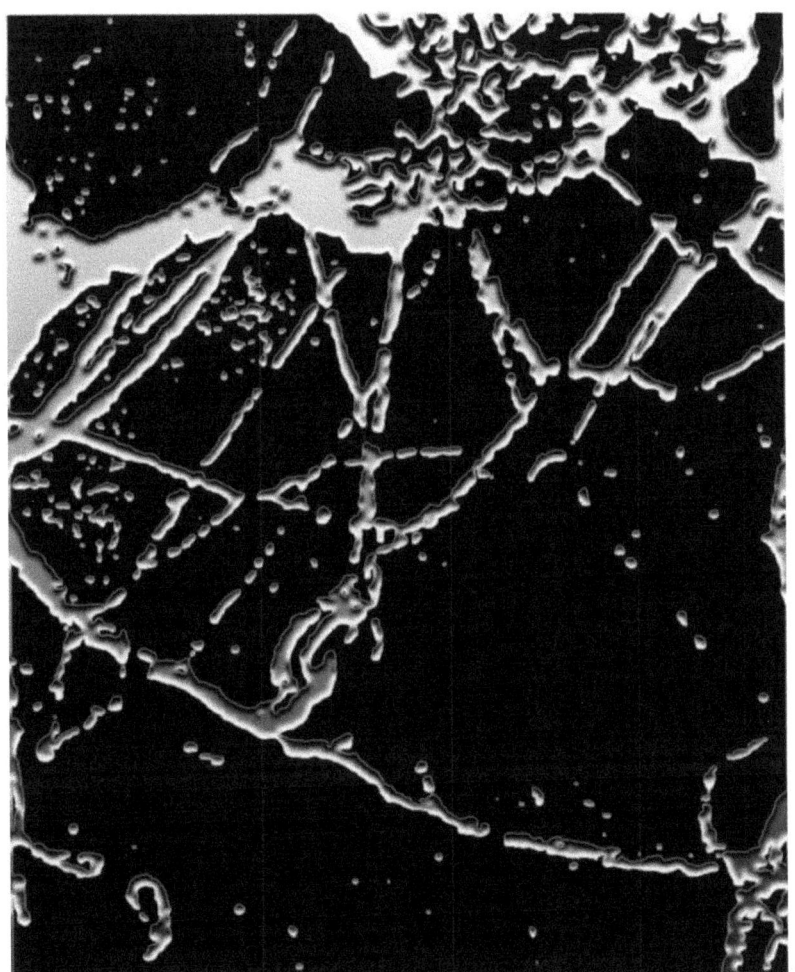

Chapter Five

Easy? Oh shit! Here we go again! Ok Molly think about this for a second. You just answered your own question.

The powers of deduction are incredible. It is a good thing I just wrote in my journal and the last experience is still fresh in my mind. The charm is in my hand, not on my bracelet, just like before. My legs are stretched out in front of me on the leg rest. Just seconds ago my legs were under my butt. The book is laying open across my lap. The picture of an empty Cavern Club is staring back at me. I can see little things in the picture that I had not noticed before. There is trash on the floor and a can, (like those Fred and Edward carried), parked by the wall. I cannot see into the tunnels. Is Fred in there sweeping?

Lin is still moving the front fender into place. I feel like I have been somewhere else for at least ten minutes. I am surprised when Lin exclaims, "Perfect on the first try! I didn't even scratch the paint. Damn I am good!"

He doesn't skip a beat. It's as if only seconds have gone by since I was silently admiring his handy work.

Let's compare trips....shall we.

1. I am not sure how long I was in Time but I know it was long enough for the bath tub to be at least half way drained yet it was still full of water. This time Lin has added a piece of sheet metal to his bike in what seems to be one fell swoop.

2. The experience of smells. Strawberry & vanilla the first time and pure high energy rock n' roll with bad ventilation this time.

3. My fingers remember touching. The curtains, the purple velvet box, then the left handed guitar and the drum stick. Oh, and that stick obviously belonged to Pete Best, since Mona his Mom was "feeding the boys", as Ed proclaimed.

4. The charm was off of my bracelet and in my hand…both times. That is definitely a common denominator.

I need to test the theory of touching the charm to start a journey. Is this the key? If I tell anyone about this experiment, will they think I am "Nucking Futs"? Why, and how, is this scenario possible? If I am really traveling to these places. What happens to my physical self while I am "gone"? Ah! New questions! You gotta love it!

It all seems so real. Way beyond anything my imagination could come up with. There is the undeniable fact, the scents did change. What if I have a medical issue that is making my brain think it is somewhere it isn't? All the more reason to test my assumption. Ok Molly, you're so damn smart, how are you going to do this?

For starters, I take off the bracelet until I have a plan.

Tomorrow is Monday. Lin has to go to work and even though he is working locally, he won't be home until late in the afternoon. Henry will be hanging out with buddies and won't return until Tuesday. If I call into work and take a vacation day, I will have the house to myself. I don't have to do payroll until Tuesday and taking one day off won't kill me. It will just make the rest of the week jammed. This is too important and I have to know now. It won't wait for the weekend.

What do I need to prove my thoughts? Where do I want to go? In the previous trips, I was thinking about the place I went to. On both trips, I travel to an empty room. There were no people around. This is a really good thing. I don't want to have to answer the question "Where did you come from"? Oh Molly, this is crazy! This is totally illogical but exciting!

Am I messing with something that I shouldn't be? I am a true believer that just because I can't explain something doesn't mean it doesn't exist. I have never seen a ghost or a spirit, but I do believe that Tim watches over our boys. I have never seen a UFO but I think it is the huge human ego that makes some people think we are the only species that exists.

My mind stops, from the spin cycle when Lin says "Molly...earth to Molly! I think I just heard Allen and Nicki pull in."

I need to write this shit down before I forget it...seriously. Timing has never been a strong point for Allen. I was in labor for 25 hours just to bring him into this world. I pick up my stuff and head for the kitchen to greet the kids and check the crock pot. Lin yells for Allen and Nicki to "come check out the '52." I take this minute to jot down a few one word notes to remind myself about my plans for tomorrow. I will come back later and fill in the blanks with details.

Dinner was awesome. The kitchen is clean. There is even enough roast left over to make up a care package for the kids to take home. It is time to relax and spend some snuggle time with Lin. We crawl into bed to snuggle (sorry no graphic details you perv, I don't kiss and tell) and watch an old war movie. True to form, Lin is sound asleep and snoring in no time. We are alike in that respect. We can watch a whole movie but, be asleep before the end of the credits. I am not even close to being tired. I go downstairs to think about my plans for tomorrow.

My journal, the laptop and my bracelet are on the kitchen table, just waiting for me. My one-word prompts are awaiting details.

Charm? – Is it the catalyst for the trips? I know both times when I came back, it was in my right hand. It wasn't broken just unclasped from the bracelet. I remember touching it the first time, I was thinking about the antique shop. I am not sure about the second time, though I was looking at the pictures in the book. I have two choices on this one. Either I am going somewhere, or I'm not. This part of the test will be easy and could possibly make my other thoughts moot.

Time? – During both trips, time seemed to stand still, or at least move very slowly. I recall the water draining and the fender being finished. If I set up a video camera tomorrow, I may see the digital time as it passes.

Seizure? – Do I have a brain tumor? If the charm test doesn't work then I need to get to the hospital. That is a scary thought! What if I am dying with some huge mass eating my brain? Did I have a seizure, or convulsions? It seems to me that if I did, Lin would have noticed in the garage. This is another little tid bit the video camera will pick up.

Pictures? – The first trip was from a mental picture and the second one was from an actual picture. In both cases, I could walk around and explore. I could touch things, pick things up, and move them. Can I go anywhere I choose by just looking at a picture?

If I am going to make another trip happen, I need to know where to go. I am not really sure I can trust my mental pictures right now. With my luck, I would end up in that "most embarrassing moment" in high school or, something stupid like that. It is a good thing that I have a laptop. Let's see what I can find...

I should go somewhere remote. I have been lucky so far. Both the shop and the pub were closed. This alleviated the "where did you come from" question. I didn't have to worry about what clothes I was wearing or fitting in. Damn there is a whole new thought...interacting with people.

Lin is poking me. What the hell? Ouch, my neck hurts. I open my eyes. Lin is up and dressed for work, standing over me with a funny look on his face. I fell asleep in the chair with the computer still on my lap. Damn, I need coffee and a shower! Lin just laughs at me as he hands me my first cup of "Joe". He also reminds me that Thomas and Poppy are coming over for dinner around six this evening.

I am awake and clean. Lin is on his way to work. It is time for me to put my plans into motion. The camera is set up in the corner of the living room pointed at the couch. It is ready to record whatever my physical self does. I am wearing a simple summer dress, nothing is hanging out and it's not too short. I look outside and everything looks peaceful so I leave the door and windows open. Give me natural air over air conditioning any day.

The laptop screen displays pictures of Arlington Cemetery. There they are, all of the beautifully lined-up white tombstones. It looks so quiet. It looks like springtime. Everything is green and there are pink cherry blossoms. There is a photo of JFK's burial site with, the eternal flame burning. There is a picture of the soldiers who performed the gun salute at his funeral. They all look like babies, lined up. Showing their respect for our fallen leader.

Ok, let's get this show on the road! The camera is rolling. I am sitting cross-legged on the couch. The computer is on the table in front of me, the pictures of the cemetery facing me. I have my bracelet on my left wrist. I begin to stare at, and think about the warm springtime pictures. Just as I reach for the charm, a car passes by and back

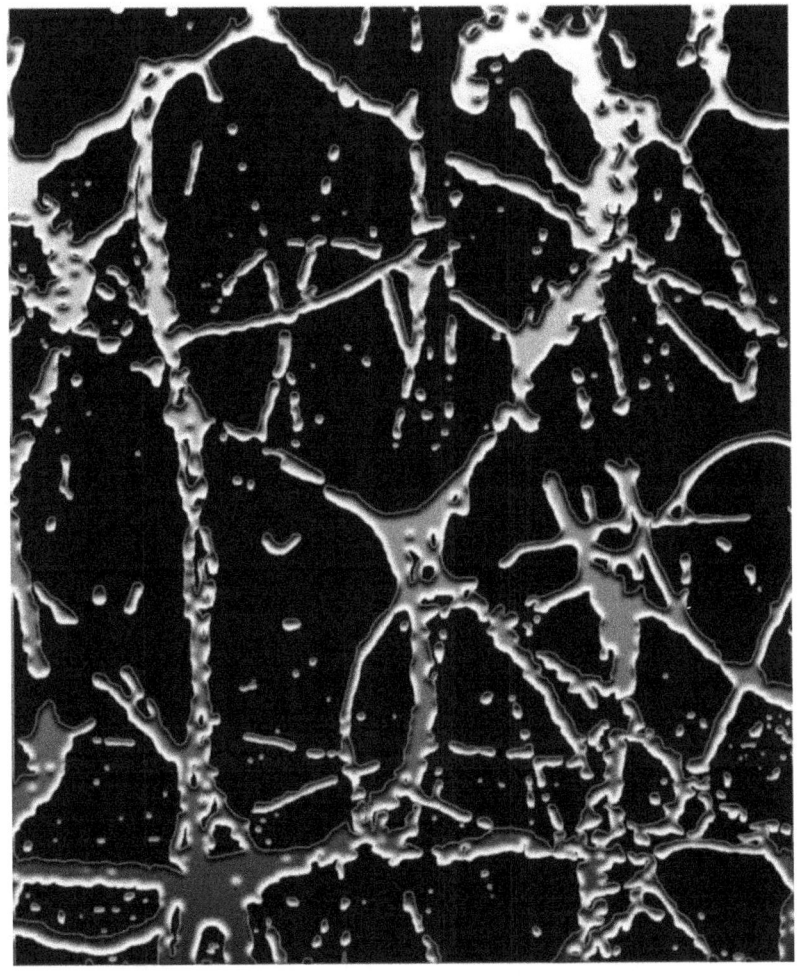

Chapter Six

Fires. Oh CRAP!!!! If this is Arlington Cemetery, why isn't it all green and peaceful? I am leaning against a very large pillar. There are a few people walking around, but no one seems to pay any attention to me. As I take a few steps forward, I hear a volley of gunfire. I am standing beside a flagpole with its proud American banner flying at half-mast. There are people as far as the eye can see in the cemetery, and what a view I have! Wow, this is incredible! I am standing in front of the Custis-Lee Mansion and this is definitely the historical resting place known as Arlington.

As I walk down the hill I notice to the left of me the ground is covered in flowers placed there by mourners. There is a small crowd of people in front of me. Everyone is very somber and silent. They seem to be the media group with the old 8mm video cameras. I see heads bobbing up and down taking pictures. No one seems to notice me, I mean at all. Everyone is wearing a coat. I even see people wrapped up in blankets. No one appears to notice or care that I am wearing just a sleeveless sun dress, which oddly enough, I am not cold. Actually, I am very comfortable.

I hear "Taps" being played on a bugle and I hear an infamous "cracked" note. Any history buff, would know that the sour note could mean I am at JFK's funeral. The location in front of the mansion is correct. If it isn't JFK's funeral, then it has to be for someone famous, with this many people here. I have to get closer to the service. I have an amazing view from here but, I want to see the faces of the family.

The question pops into my head. What if no one can see me? How fucking cool would that be? This would explain why no one has made eye contact with me or pointed at the crazy lady who should be freezing.

I have to move fast and check out my theory. I see a little old lady standing beside me. She reminds me of Aunt Bea but this isn't Mayberry. She is intently staring straight ahead. I am 5'11" tall, so I stand right in front of her blocking her view completely with my shoulders and chest. I get no reaction, no sour look, and no request for me to move. I get nothing. Aunt Bea continues to watch the ceremony. Holy Shit! I am invisible. I wave my arms like I'm a chicken on an acid trip and still nothing. That's all the proof I need…

I take off running further down the hill, aiming to the left for the "not too many people" section. I have got to haul ass, Taps is almost finished. I make it down without incident. I am 100% sure no one can see me. If all of these military dudes can see a crazy women running down the hill towards them, how long do you think it would take before I am lying on my belly with men sitting on me?

I sneak up and stand beside a man wearing a white headpiece. It looks similar to a nun's habit with a tall hat underneath it, and a long white train down his back. I see many dignitaries. There is Charles De Gaulle, looking like a very sad and stoic Inspector Clouseau. I see the Emperor of Ethiopia, Haile Salassie. He is in his dress uniform with many medals and a bright green sash across his chest. I see so many faces of people I have only read about and seen in history books, sharing the same emotion of grief. To my right is the Kennedy family. Jean, Pat, Rose, and Eunice, the whole family is here. Jackie, Bobby, and Teddy walk past me to move to the end of the casket. Pictures don't give justice to the sad look I see on Jackie's face. All three of them look completely consumed by pain and sorrow.

In front of me, every branch of the military is represented. They are standing alongside the coffin, at attention holding an American flag above our 35th president. Next they fold the flag in military fashion. Once it reaches its final triangle shape, it is given, with a salute, to an older man with white hair. He takes a couple steps and hands it to Jackie. He says a few words to her and Bobby, but I can't hear what he is saying. Jackie takes a step towards the casket and is handed a torch. Her delicate form leans forward and lights the eternal flame. She turns and hands the torch to Bobby, who does the same thing. Bobby turns to his left, then realizes Teddy is on his right. Teddy steps up and also touches the torch to the flame. After Bobby hands the flame back to a solider, he takes Jackie by the hand, and they walk away from their loved one.

The family falls in line behind Bobby and Jackie. Then the crowd starts to close in on me. Thank God everyone is moving really slowly. Something tells me I have to get out of the way….fast. I make a path to the flowers laid out on the hill. If I stand in the middle of them, I won't get walked on. That makes sense.

One thing I notice is color. I have seen this historical event on television but it was always in black and white. The flowers are so beautiful; red, white, and yellow. I have been to see JFK's grave but, it was after it had been moved just a few feet from where it is now. It is so sad that I know Bobby and Jackie will join JFK here in the years to come. One life snuffed out way to early, and the other lived with tormenting memories. I am amazed that so many people can be in one place and the silence be so deafening.

I sit down among the flowers and think about what I have just witnessed. I am overcome with emotion. I don't think I have any tears left to cry. The hem of my dress is covered with mascara, tears, and snot. I watch as most of the cars leave the cemetery. I reach down and untangle a ribbon from a flower wreath. It says "We won't forget you". I tie the ribbon around my ankle in a bow. I could really go for a cigarette right now. Note to self: put smokes in your pocket.

It is getting late and I am ready to go home. I have been here at least a couple of hours. If my theory is correct, I need to remove the charm from the bracelet to return home. Ok, here we go! On your mark, get set…

Chapter Seven

Go.

It takes me just a split second to realize my theory worked. I am sitting cross legged on the couch looking at the video cameras red blinking light. The room is the same. Nothing has changed. The computer is on the table, lit up with the pictures of Arlington Cemetery. How can that be? The computer should be dark after a few minutes of no activity. One way to find out; let's roll tape.

As I get up off the couch to push play, I notice the ribbon tied around my ankle. I plop back down as if someone has pushed me in the chest. I untie the ribbon and sure enough, there are the words "We won't forget you".

Oh shit! This is big, cool, scary and the most exciting thing that has ever happened to me. Think of the things I can learn first-hand. I can witness so many incredible events in history. Reading about things in the past involves two things: sight (reading the words) and imagination. How lucky am I that I can see, smell, taste, feel and hear all of this cool shit? Right now I feel a little physically drained. I need a nap or a shot of caffeine. I opt for a Diet Pepsi since I have a video to watch. I couldn't sleep now if I wanted to. My mind is going a hundred miles an hour with all of the wonderful possibilities.

Time for playback. There I am, looking at the pictures on the computer. I hear a loud car go by just as I touch the charm. Does this explain how I ended up at the funeral for JFK? My body does not move. I am holding the charm between my fingers. The only portion of my body that does move are my eyes. I close them. I don't notice a change in my breathing. It all seems very peaceful and relaxing. I remain motionless until my fingers unclasp the charm and my eyes open.

The timer on the video shows a little over two minutes has gone by. How can that be? I was at the cemetery for at least two hours. This leaves one question unanswered without more research. Maybe I need to wear a stopwatch and compare it to a clock present during my travels. Does one minute of reality equal one hour of travel? Is that the ratio?

One question has been answered by the ribbon: I am not suffering from a medical condition. Brain tumors don't create objects from nothing and I don't appear to have any outward reactions. I have also figured out that the charm is the key to the journeys. I have new observations and questions to record in my journal.

1. Obviously, I remember the trips. I also seem to bring the emotion back to the present with me. When I got back from Arlington, I actually felt the exhaustion one feels after a long period of crying. My dress is a mess to prove it.

2. I have figured out I'm invisible. Does this mean I can go anywhere without dealing with people? Can they feel me if I bump into them? I must have some mass if I can pick up things and move them. Why and how did the ribbon come back with me?

3. It appears that I can use a picture to choose my destination. I think my subconscious thoughts play a part in this too. If my brain had not heard the car backfire would my trip have gone as planned? What about a time before cameras? Can I use a painting?

4. Can I make an effect while I travel? I will have to be cognizant not to change history. There has to be a domino effect. OMG! Just think about that for a second!

5. If I go back and change the mistakes I have made along the way in my life, what does that do to my future and the people I love? Would that change the person I am?

All of this could make a person go stark raving mad! It could also be the best damn adventure ever created. I have two choices: I can either take the charm back to the shop to tell ole boy thanks, but no thanks and go on with my life as is or I can figure out how this works. I could write a book about history from a front row seat. The thought of that makes my whole body tingle with caged excitement.

Before I make a decision, I need to get some of my questions answered and learn more about the man who gave me this choice to make. Why did he give away this beautiful opportunity? Why did he choose me? What can I learn from him? This is where a computer will come in handy.

The shop "Time" was opened in 1953 by Dmitri Kossak. The brief history says Mr. Kossak came to this country from Poland as a boy of 12 with his parents. His father took their life savings and a family inheritance to purchase the two story building. It became a successful dry goods store. The second floor was the home of the family. Dmitri's parents were killed in an accident in 1952 and the shop was left to him as their only child. After renovations, Dmitri opened an antique shop. He was 23 years old. There are a couple of pictures of the Grand Opening. Dmitri is definitely the man who gave me the charm. I am amazed at how tall and handsome he looks. His smile lights up the black and white photo of him with his wife, Anna.

I hear Lin pull into the driveway, home from his day at work. I can't believe I have been sitting here all day. The ash tray is over flowing with butts. I see six empty pop cans. That's funny I don't remember going pee today. I have filled out a dozen pages in my journal and my eyes are burning from looking at a computer screen too long. Oh shit! I have got to think of something quick. The kids will be here in an hour. I hope Lin thinks Chinese food sounds good.

He walks into the room and I can tell by his "don't fuck with me" look, he has not had a good day.

"How was your day, Baby?" I ask.

"Where do you want me to begin? The cup of coffee I have been wearing all day or the idiot oiler that wouldn't know a proper hand signal if Helen Keller herself taught him. I made six picks with my piece of shit crane today. The last one I had to hold for almost two hours while a dork in the front office went over the blueprints again. That stupid son of a bitch wouldn't know if he should wind his ass or scratch his watch. Don't even get me started about the suits that came to the worksite today. How was your day and what's for supper? The kids will be here soon and you know they'll be hungry."

Now comes my time to confess that I have made no plans for food, other then ordering out.

"Are you kidding me Molly? I'm glad you enjoyed your day off. By the looks of it, you are working on some project but you could have at least taken five minutes to throw something in the oven for shits sake. I'm going to go take a shower."

Lin is not a demanding or an angry man, unless he is hungry. All bets are off when he needs to eat. As he has said many times "If ya want me to be a dick, just don't feed me." While he is decompressing in a stream of warm water I call in the Chinese delivery. Since we are all creatures of habit, I know the order by heart, including what Thomas and Poppy will want.

This adds another question to my journal. Can I take on this adventure and still be a good mom, wife and- for now- employee? I really need to give Dmitri a visit pretty damn quick. What can I learn from him, the "young him"?

We have a nice dinner with the kids. We even kick their asses in a couple games of beer pong in the garage. Back in our day we played a game called Quarters. That was much harder than this carnival fish bowl game. I do get a heartfelt apology from Lin about being such a prick when he got home. He does have a point, I dropped the ball. I wait until all is quiet and he has fallen asleep before I give Mr. Kossak a visit. Must learn balance Grasshopper.

Lin starts snoring not long after his head hits the pillow. Thank you, beer pong. I quietly get out of bed and gather up what I need for my trip. The beauty of being invisible is a very nice perk. I am going in my boxer shorts and an over-sized t-shirt. I have my stopwatch around my neck: I am sitting comfortably on the couch and looking at the pictures of "Time" from 1953. It is 9:37 pm according to my cell phone and the computer.

I wonder if Dmitri will sense my presence. It's almost like I am

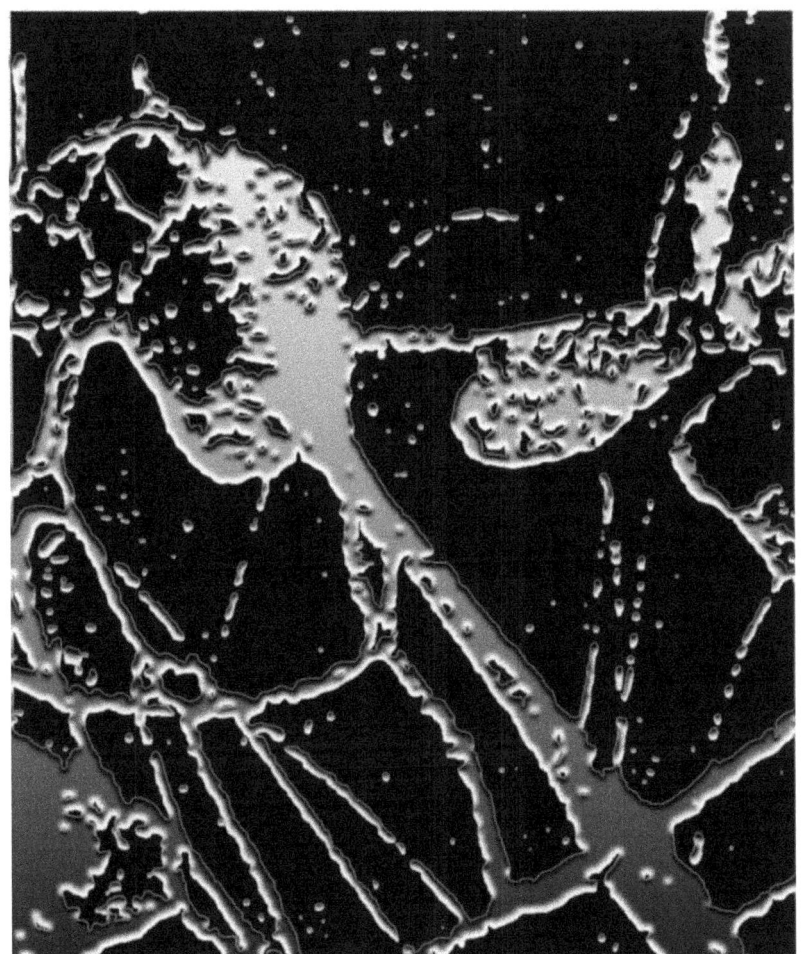

Chapter Eight

Haunting him. There is no flash of light; no sense of flying or motion at all for that matter. It feels like opening a car door and stepping out into a different world. I push the button on the stopwatch. I am where I want to be and there stands Dmitri with his lovely wife, getting their picture taken for the newspapers. This is definitely not the "age of digital". The camera is huge and when the flash goes off there is a pop with a small puff of smoke. Hey, I remember that smell!

The ladies are all wearing hats and simple cotton dresses that go down to the mid-calf. No cleavage here folks! Blouses are buttoned clear to the top. I see a few women wearing white gloves. The men are wearing suits complete with a hat and tie. No one seems to be in a big hurry to get to where they are going. The hoopla going on with the Kossaks seems to be of great entertainment. Imagine that, at home everyone is taking pictures left and right with their cell phones. When was the last time I stopped to watch someone take a picture?

I am standing in front of the shop, which looks very different. When Lin and I were here, the only portion used was the basement. Now the first floor (street level) is the store, and according to the sign in the window "Antiques from all different places in "Time". That's a clever play on words. The front door is open and what a sight to behold. The walls are lined with the magnificent shelves I saw on my first trip. They are shiny and new, covered with all kinds of antiques. This is not a junk shop, everything here is exquisite and high-class. Mr. Kossak must have been collecting this stuff for years. There are many beautiful things that I would love to have. I see a clock behind the register counter that tells me it is 5:17. I am alone, with the exception of Dmitri and Anna, who have just walked in. He closes and locks the front door. They both seem very excited about the announcement that is going to run in the local paper. They are not speaking English, so I can't tell what they are saying, but the smiles and the laughter tell me all that I need to know.

Anna opens a door behind the counter and walks up the stairs with Dmitri close on her heels. I decide to bring up the rear. At the top of the stairs is a nice living room area. The furniture must have come with the apartment. It looks old, well-loved and comfy. I do not see a television, but there is a radio on the table between two chairs. It reminds me of visiting my great grandparents' house. I follow the Kossaks into the kitchen where dinner is waiting for them. Anna puts on an apron and takes two plates out of the oven. What a great kitchen! It is very clean, simple, and organized. I do like the nice shade of pale yellow with white trimmings.

While they eat, I am going to explore.

Down a little hallway is the master bedroom, another small room that looks like Anna has set up for sewing, and a very pink bathroom. The rooms aren't real big, but they are all clean, warm, homey and comfortable. I do not see a nursery or any indication that Dmitri and Anna have children. The rooms all look too clean and organized to have kids running around. Since Dmitri is an antique dealer, I would expect to see old things everywhere, but I don't. The decorations aren't sparse. They are all uncluttered and simple memories. There are lots of books and old family photos. Lying on the table is a newspaper dated April 18, 1953 with the headline "Mantle slams record HR Giants split; Yanks win". Wow the Mantle/Maris race isn't until 1961. Henry and Allen would shit a brick if they knew I was standing here reading a new press release about Mickey Mantle.

I am startled out of my reading mind by Dmitri "Ah so you are da next one"?

I look at him and he is looking at the mirror in front of me. I look at my reflection in the mirror and he is staring into my eyes. Of course I see myself but this is completely wild. He can see me! I hear Anna walking out of the kitchen. "Dmitri who are you talking to", she asks.

"Just tinking out loud. I am going downstairs to lock up while you finish da cleaning" he says.

He looks at me after Anna walks back into the kitchen and wiggles his finger for me to follow. We both walk down the stairs.

After Dmitri closes the door, he tells me, "Get into da mirror dere so I can see you".

He points in the direction of an old dressing mirror in the corner of the shop. He doesn't seem to be surprised, shocked or startled in the least. It is almost like he had been expecting me. I walk to the mirror and once we have made eye contact I finally find my voice and say "Hello".

In a very amused calmness, he explains "I cannot hear you but yes I see you and I do know how you got here. No worries, I am da only one who can see you. Only dose who have worked da charm can see you as a reflection. You will have to write down your questions. If I know da answer, I will tell you. Den it will be my turn to ask you".

I find a pen on the counter and write on the palm of my hand. Who would have guessed in a million years that a trick I learned in high school would ever come in handy and useful? I write my three questions backwards so Dmitri can read them in the mirror.

1. Why me?
2. Harmful?
3. Secrets of the charm?

I hold up my hand for Dmitri to read. He rubs his chin with a smile, almost a smirk.

"In my day, if you wrote wit your left hand you got smacked wit a ruler. Let me tell you my story and answer your questions as I go please."

"My parents died a year ago in an unfortunate accident. On da day of da funeral, I was approached by a very old woman who asked me of my momma's charm bracelet. Dis was an odd inquiry, but yes my momma did own a very old bracelet and I told her dis. She asked me to bring it to her da next day at a local coffee shop. Dis woman said no more and walked away from me. I went to meet her and I find out her name is Clara. Her family comes from Germany, but she was born in da United States and she is 87 years old."

"Clara tells me dat she has a gift for me dat, I am da chosen one, but she had to wait until da bracelet came into my possession. So my dear, you are also da chosen one" he continues to explain.

"Now dat I have seen your face I will know you in da future, just as Clara knew me. Just as you are doing now. I traveled back to meet a younger Clara. Dat is a very pleasant memory for me."

"Is dis harmful you ask? Look around you. I have all of dis because of my travels. Anyting dat you can hold will travel forward wit you. There are many secrets, and most of dem you will have to learn on your own, as I am. I have learned you can go back in time using a mental picture or a visual aid as you touch da charm. You cannot travel into da future. Be careful with your heart and history. I visited my parents and my very soul ached for weeks. Now comes my time to ask. Am I old when you get da charm from me? Is Anna dere? Do we meet here in da shop?"

I lick my hand and wipe it on my shirt so I can start with a clean slate.

1. You are 82

2. No I don't see her

3. Yes basement

Dmitri seems surprised by my answers.

"Ah I make it to da new century. I hope my Anna is dere too. Speaking of Anna, I have to leave you now she is waiting for me upstairs. Stay as long as you like. Please come visit me again. I may have more questions and answers for you. What is your name" he asks.

Again, with the magic spit, I clean my hand and write "MOLLY". Dmitri gives me a bow and says "Goodbye for now, Molly."

I stick around for a little while and look at the treasures Dmitri has in his shop. Now it makes sense, everything here is no bigger than one person can carry. I think about the ribbon on my ankle. I didn't hold it in my hands when it traveled with me. What if anything that touches my skin can travel? I decide to test my theory. I am going to take back the mirror in the corner. Now I could pick it up, but that would not prove my point. In true Molly fashion, I shoot the moon in front of the mirror and touch it with my ass. I look at the clock and it says 7:12. I have been here almost exactly two hours. Just

.

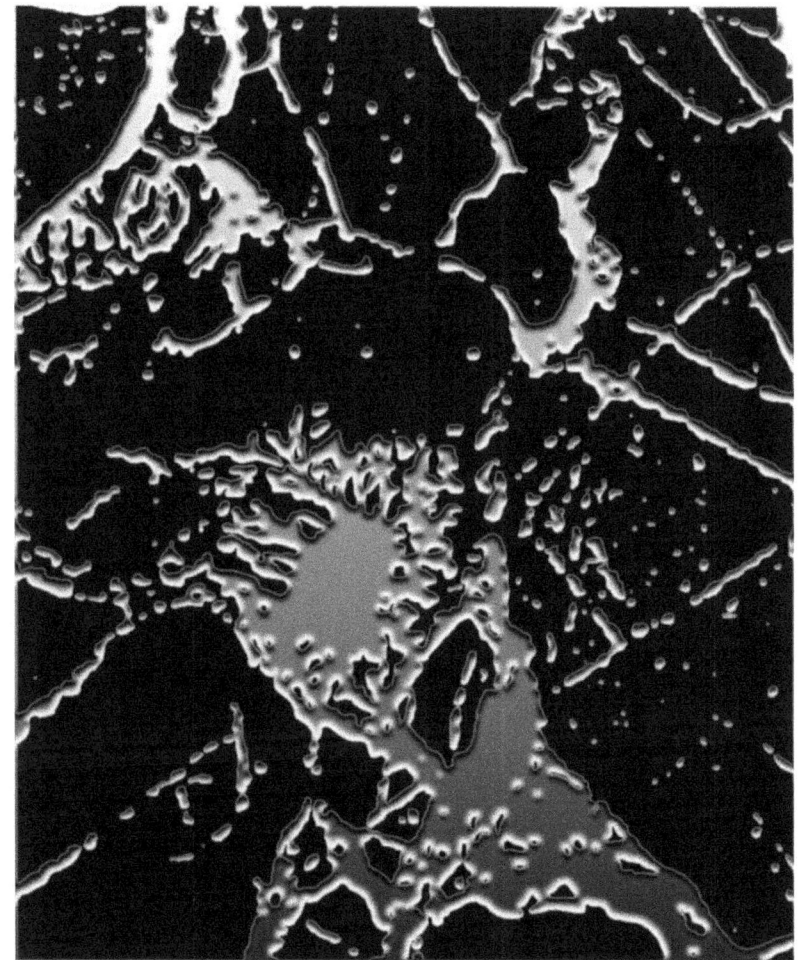

Chapter Nine

Imagine all the treasures I could collect if my theory is correct.

I am back home and yes, the mirror is touching my ass. What Dmitri hasn't figured out is that it is not what you can carry but, what touches your skin that travels with you. How fucking cool it that? Oh wow I have really got to be careful in the future; no leaning on the Lincoln monument when I touch the charm! That would be really hard to explain to Lin. Not to mention, how in the hell would I get it out of my living room?

Suddenly I remember the stop watch around my neck. I punch the button and it has passed just a little over two minutes. Ok, a second theory is proved. One minute in reality is one hour in the past. The clock on the wall says 9:40.

It is time to write down what I have learned. The whole business about being seen as a reflection but not being heard is strange. Dmitri even assumes I am left handed, having not realized that everything in the mirror is reversed. The fact that I can choose where I travel has been confirmed and subconscious thought does play a part in it. I will have to think about going back to see Tim, Kitt or my parents. Can my heart take it? I miss all of them so much that sometimes when I think about them my chest physically aches from the inside. Most of the time I can think back with a smile but every once in awhile it deeply hurts. Is that fair to Henry, Allen and Lin?

I am exhausted to the point of not being able to hold a thought anymore. My mind is racing from one scenario to the next, without a pit stop. I snuggle into bed beside my sweet Lin. This is my favorite place in the world. Spooning is so under-rated for its calming properties.

I wake up to Lin waving a cup of coffee under my nose. He sits down beside me and says "Where did the cool antique mirror come from"? That makes my eyes pop open! Oh shit! Think fast, Molly. I tell him that it was delivered yesterday and it was from my Aunt Suzy. Note to self: call Aunt Suzy to tell her it was from her and to play along if Lin asks. This is why I hate lying about anything. It is way too much work for my brain to remember who I told what lie to. If you tell the truth, you don't have to waste brain juice, just keep the factual memories stored. I will have to remedy this. Right off the bat, I have stolen a mirror and lied to Lin. I don't like this feeling. There is a line in a song that says "An honest man's pillow is his peace of mind". That phrase has always struck a chord in me. I will have to take the mirror back, or at least pay for it. Both solutions require an explanation to Dmitri.

As for the lie, that is another matter to be given some serious thought. I can't tell Lin the truth. My conscience tells me omission of facts, is just as much a lie as making up some cock 'n bull story. The only solution, for right now is to be discreet and respectful. No more verbal lies to Lin.

Michael and Eric are both in the office today. This doesn't happen much anymore. They are both in rare form and coming up with projects for me to do. Now mind you, I love my job, but doing everyday "make-the-business-go" functions keeps me plenty busy without any extra projects. I cannot deny I do love the challenge, but over the years I have picked up on most of what they are going to ask for before they do. Ya gotta love spreadsheets! Thank you Bill Gates.

It is hard to stay on task. All I want to do is daydream about taking a trip. When do I want to go? Do I want to visit a king? Do I want to see a kick ass band in concert? There are countless possibilities. How do I correct my lie? Cheese and rice! Is this day ever going to end? I want to go home and make a plan.

I beat Lin home and whip up a casserole that needs to bake for an hour. Just as I pop a beer and finish a bump, Allen and Nicki pull in. Good thing I am making enough for four if I throw in biscuits and a side of fruit. By the looks on their faces this is not a "how ya doing Mom?" visit. Whew, here comes my knight in a shiny truck. Lin pulls into the driveway.

The kids get very serious once we get something to drink and sit down outside. Allen breaks the silence when he tells me that I am about to become a grandmother. My reaction is not one of surprise, but there is this little voice that says "Damn Mol, you are getting old."

I slide into silent thought mode while eating my dinner. Oddly enough all four of us seem to be chewing in a hushed quiet. The kids are young adults, not high school students, so old enough to figure it out. I can only tell them what I have learned and point them in the right direction. The rest is up to them. It is what it is.

I am excited about having a grandchild. I envision my grand babies coming to stay at my house in the summers for weeks at a time. While I am not surprised, I can't say I am ready for this one. It doesn't change my plans of moving with Lin. It actually makes me more eager, I want the change in my life to happen sooner rather than later. There is some comfort in the fact that Nicki and Allen are down to earth, good people. Young and ignorant, yes, but they are not stupid. I think they will be good parents and learn along the way, like we all do at one time or another. I will be a good grandma, but I will do it by my rules, in my own way, with lots of love.

After the kids leave and we settle into "veg" mode, I start thinking about my plan. What can I do with my newfound ability that may enable me to quit my job? Looking at finances, if I paid off the house I could become gainfully unemployed. I don't want to steal. I could go back and buy something from Dmitri, but it would have to be something he hasn't stolen. I am not passing judgment on Dmitri. That is his adventure and his cross to bear, not mine. I don't want to invent something. That would be changing history, wouldn't it? I could go back and invest in a sure-fire stock, but that would be cheating. I don't want to be rich beyond my wildest dreams. I want to be free to enjoy this special gift and do it while flying under the radar.

My mind keeps coming back to the thought that I need to buy, find, or be given a historical artifact or some sort of memorabilia that I can bring back with me to sell. I can't tell Lin where this found money comes from. Shit, how can I do this without lying? There has to be a way to find a discarded famous signature. This will take some research. Lin and I are going to a swap meet this weekend. I usually find a nice quiet spot to sit and read while he looks for old bike shit.

The rest of the week at work confirms my desire to get this show on the road. I am not looking forward to telling Eric and Michael. They have been good to me and my family. I think they will get along just fine without me. They should have no problem replacing me. I can't help but feel like I am letting down a friend. Every spare moment this week has been spent exploring my trip options.

Now the weekend is finally here and we are on our way to the swap meet. My man is in a good mood and ready for the almighty quest of old bike parts. Hence the small trailer attached to the back of my vehicle. Lin never seems to come home empty handed.

I have a premeditated destination. I have decided to kill two birds with one stone. I'm not sure about part of this plan, but it will test another theory.

Lin is in his element and happier than a hog in shit. I can't get angry with him when he barely notices me walk off to find my secluded spot. I do the same thing to him in museums. I always seem to get sucked into the moment. I become deaf and lack peripheral vision. Run, you clever boy, go find your parts.

I see a row of trees away from the beaten path and spread out my blanket. I strategically place an open book in my lap so if anyone walks by I look like I am reading. It is quiet here so distractions shouldn't be a factor. I have everything I think I will need in an over-the-shoulder tote bag. I hope it can travel with me, because theoretically it is not touching my skin. This trip has taken a lot of planning. Hopefully, there aren't too many bumps in the road. I have my thoughts set on a mental picture of where I am going. All systems are 'go'. As Alan Shepard said "Light this candle." It is

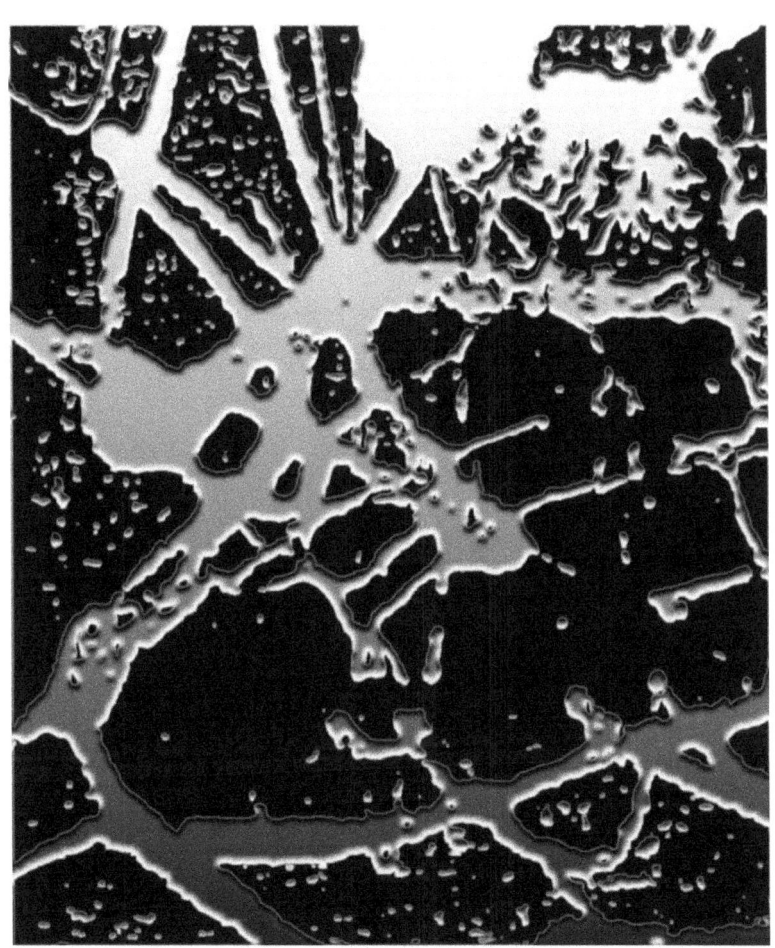

Chapter Ten

Just a blink of the eye. Damn I am getting good at this. Way cool! The bag can travel! I will have to test the theory of putting something in the bag. Will it travel with me too?

I am back in Dmitri's shop. I have written him a note explaining what I have learned about bringing things back by sheer touch. I have included his $30.00 asking price. It was not fun trying to find "old" money. I can't give him a bill printed after 1953. That would just be stupid on so many levels. I hope he didn't steal the mirror. I don't like pleading ignorance; in most cases it is just a cop-out. Unfortunately, I have put myself in a position with Lin in which I have no choice but to pay for it, and learn what I don't want to repeat. I trust Dmitri will find the envelope, not Anna, or he may have some explaining to do. There isn't much light so in order to attempt part two of this journey, I have to pull out a penlight from my tote to see my next destination. If you know what happened for three days in June 1967, you know where I am going. I just hope my research pays off.

I retrieve a picture I printed from a website. It is backstage at the Monterey Pop Festival. According to my research, this is where the performers would hang out and have a "cocktail" as the sign advertises. There are so many talented and infamous people here. I am bound to find something that I can make a nickel on. God I hate money. It truly is the root of all evil. Is there anything else in the world that will make a human being turn into a greedy, self serving, immoral, lying asshole quicker? I think not. I am not going to make this "trip for money" a habit. It kinda makes me feel dirty. I touch the charm and "POOF", we are in Monterey California. Star date 1967.

WHOA! Fuck me running! There is Grace Slick and Mama Cass. Walking towards me is David Crosby. Mickey Dolenz is in a feather headdress and holding up a wall is Mr. Brian Jones, wearing a really frilly pink cape. I perk up my ears to hear Simon and Garfunkel singing "Homeward Bound". I can't even explain what I am feeling right now. I am buzzing from the inside out with excitement and a rush of energy. I want to soak in as much as I can.

Speaking of "soaking", someone here has some really good-smelling weed. I think I need to follow my nose and walk through that cloud of smoke a couple of times. I gotta get my head right to be here in true form. Oh yeah, a nice little head adjustment. Just my luck. I get to catch the over-flow of a powerful shotgun. I am here to tell you my friends, the weed in the 60's is much better than anything I can get back home. It is an instant "pump me up" buzz not, a "melt into the couch" buzz. Now, let's explore and see what I can find.

Damn, this is too fucking cool for words! I don't see any signs of violence or anger. Everyone is just mellow and enjoying the peace of the music. I see a young couple carrying a sleeping child. I see cops with flowers in their hats and on their uniforms. I giggle to myself thinking about a Twisted Sister video. Oh, shut up Niedermeyer!

I know it is cliché, but I feel the love. There is not even an inkling of hatred or ugliness. Before I go check out the audience up close and personal. I'm going to go mingle with some faces I have only read about. I want to find Janis. I am a sucker for a strong female voice. They don't get much stronger than the pipes on Janis.

I don't want to go to the "Hunt Club/Green Room" right now. The thought of Tiny Tim is a major buzz kill. My research has told me that he likes to hang out there holding court. I'm sorry, but I don't think I could ever get so stoned to think that sounds good. I am sure he is a kind soul, but wow, talk about sounding like a cat getting raped. I am going to check out the actual "backstage/sidestage".

What a beautiful feast for my ears. The song "Sounds of Silence". I look around and notice I am not the only one who feels the tranquility of this song. Garfunkel starts out rough, but it takes him only a few seconds to sound like an angel. The whole backstage, and the audience for that matter, is being swallowed up by this succulent ear candy. I am afraid to move for fear I will make a noise that would interrupt this peace.

As soon as they start "Benedictus"…I emerge from my trance and get back on task. I leave the dark side of the stage. I see Janis sitting against the wall. I notice she has a pad of paper on her lap. It looks like she is doodling or writing a letter, off in her own world.

It seems like most of the people are breaking off into smaller groups and moving their parties somewhere else. Oh yeah, me thinks there will be some jamming tonight! It is hard to walk around and purposely try not to bump into anyone or anything.

I hear Janis giggle and turn around to see her pop up on her feet, which her dog isn't real happy about. I don't recognize the dude she is talking to. I am too far away to hear what they are saying. After passing the Soco back and forth a couple times she takes him by the arm and off they go.

Low and behold there is a balled up piece of paper on the floor. I can't just pick it up and unfold it. I know these people are fucked up but I think someone might notice a piece of paper straightening out in mid air all by itself. There is another theory to test: what actions are visible to anyone looking? I go over and kick the ball of paper into a secluded corner, quickly pick it up, and shove it into my tote bag.

The music is over for now, at least the stage performances anyway. Time to go outside and see what I can find. The festival is my oyster. I wonder around the grounds. What a cool set-up! I see vendors selling crystals, jewelry, candles and munchies. I see people making out everywhere. I see a huge ass teepee. I think this is where you go if you find yourself on a bad acid trip. Outside the venue there is a small city of hippies all spread out enjoying the music free of charge. The vibe is the same out here. "Peace, love and whatever baby".

There are people sleeping on the local high school football field, all curled up in blankets and sleeping bags. I want to see Big Brother and the Holding Company with Janis perform later today. It may be dark but, it is now Saturday. I am not here to sleep, I can do that at home.

Back inside the festival grounds you can hear a jam session going on. My ears lead me to the Hunt Club. I don't hear Tiny Tim, so I think I am safe in that regard. I see Paul Simon, Jimi Hendrix, Paul Butterfield, David Crosby and John Entwistle, each contributing to the music. Again, I am trying not to get giddy about the legends I see. Every direction or turn of my head gives me another famous face. It is sad to know that a few of these beautiful souls will be gone soon, way before they should be. "Better to burn out than to fade away".

It is easier to find a spot against the wall or a corner than it is to wiggle in between the people. I have already made Country Joe McDonald spill a whole drink. Good thing he is really fucked up and blames it on someone else. No harsh words though, he is given a replacement and all is good. The confrontation ends with a "right on man. Let's party."

I need to get back on task and accomplish what I came here to do. So far I have found an un-used ticket on the ground and a small poster that I pulled out of the trash. Here is the problem. I see all kinds of things lying around that are part of this historical event, but nothing of tangible proof. I could go pick up the piece of chewing gum that Jimi just spit into the trash but to prove it was in his mouth would take a DNA test. I see a few problems with that. Is there anything in the future to compare it to? Do I really want to go to all the bother? The questions would be: How I got it and where has been all of these years? This is some tricky, could be gross, shit! I have some time to kill so I settle in, sit back to listen, think and observe. Maybe I will get lucky and see something other than a broken guitar string or an empty bottle being tossed out.

While the energy is up in the room it is easy to pass the time but once things start slowing down and there are only a few people staggering around, it is time to move back outside.

"Here comes the sun little darling. Here comes the sun and I say it's alright". I head back towards the stage. There is John Phillips making plans for the day and shouting out orders. The sound guys are hard at it. There are a bunch of busy bees taking care of business. I see teenagers wiping off chairs, picking up trash and helping on the stage. I don't think the gates are open yet or this place would be packed to the gills with people. OMG is that Mr. Steve Miller doing a sound check? This is going to be a good day. I have no idea what time it is, but then who cares? I am going to stay for Janis. I need to find a spot so I can enjoy the show. Some place out of the way, by the speakers of course.

Hey, I still have that ball of paper in my bag. I need to find the restroom before all hell breaks loose and see what I have.

I have to go into the men's room since there is a team of plumbers in the women's. Cool, an empty bathroom with an open stall. I dig out my "pay off the house" fodder. I hope this is something really amazing, because I don't have much. It's not crunched up too tight so I'm good there. Oh Yeah! Come to momma! It is doodles and drawings. The best part: in the corner she has written her full name "Janis Lyn Joplin". Below her name is a drawing that says "Monterey Pop Festival 1967". I am not an expert on the value but this has got to be good. By George (John, Paul and Ringo) I think I've done it!

Oh shit! I hear men coming in. I walk out and there are three guys. I'll be damned if one of them doesn't look just like Harrison Ford (pre Han Solo). Hmmm, go figure. Time to go, it is not a fetish of mine to watch men take a piss.

It has to be getting close to show time. The gates must be open because the midway is getting full. It is amazing to see such a diverse group of people. I see preppy college students, soldiers, hippies just getting here and people trying to shake off yesterday to start all over again today. I think the heart and soul of the vibrations here is the fact that the music doesn't stop. Even when there isn't anyone on stage there is music piped in. I need to get my head right before the festivities begin. Talk about being a kid in a candy store.

Perfect timing, I am snuggled into my spot in between the speakers. Time for some Canned Heat y'all. Let's do a little "Rollin & Tumblin". Janis is in the wings. She looks as nervous as a 16-year old boy buying condoms. In the future, women with beautiful voices feel the need to make it all about "how much skin can I show" instead of letting their music be their offering. That is one thing I always admired about Janis. Is she dolled up? Yes, but her shit isn't hanging out. If you want to show off your tits, go ahead. There are magazines for that. You wanna make music just open your mouth and leave the rest of the crap to people who can't sing.

In between sets…I take the opportunity to leave my hidey-hole and take a bump off of a long neck bong that has been left unattended. Doing that without making it move is a challenge in itself. It is a good thing there is still fire in the hole. The cylinder is not see- through, so filling it up with smoke for a tasty release is not a problem. Good thing I cannot be heard, ya don't get off unless you cough.

Oh shit here we go. I hear her "straight from the tips of her toes" chant "Down on me". This is almost beyond what I can handle! Think about it. I am hearing, seeing and feeling the vibrations rattle my ribcage off the speakers of this gut-wrenching, reach-down-and-pull-it-up-to-slap-it-in-your-face voice. I am in such an awesome place right now. I don't want it to end.

I want to stay for Country Joe and the Fish, but I have to get back. I have been gone for at least 16 hours. I can't take a chance with the piece of paper not traveling back with me so I pick up one of the flowers on the stage and put it in the bag. Man I am really going to miss the good

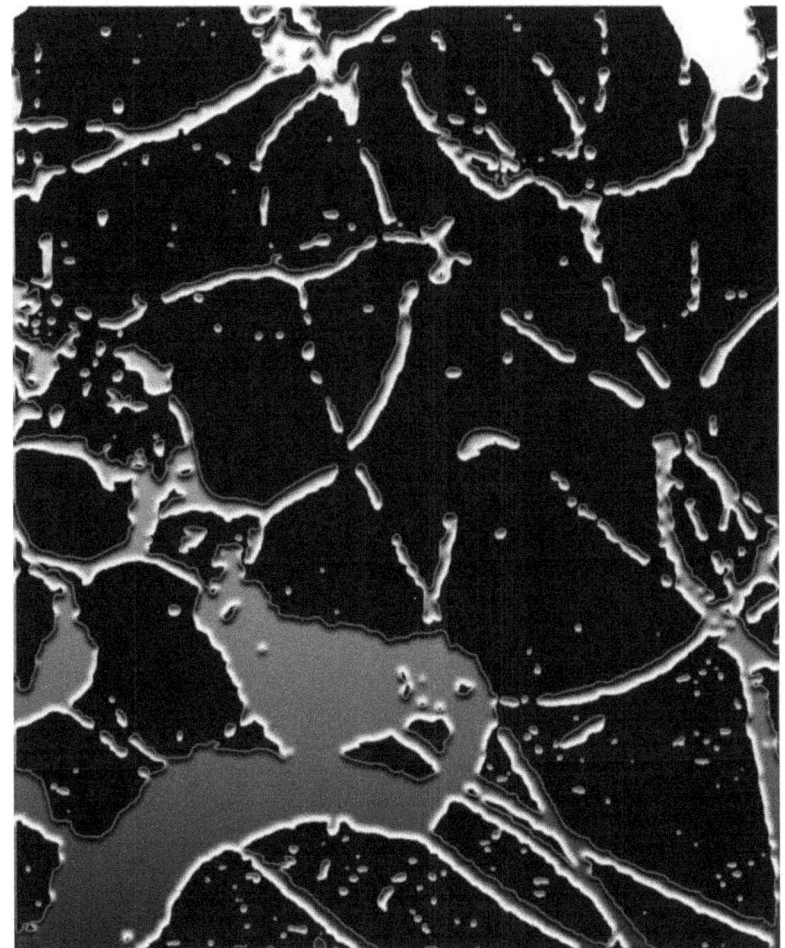

Chapter Eleven

Karma here. I am just where I should be, sitting on my blanket.

The ticket and my treasure are in hand. I lift up my dress, and tucked under my garter belt is the rolled up poster. I dump out my bag, alas no flower. Man, I'm glad I didn't take a chance with the good shit. I need to go find Lin and let him know where I am. That way, I can come back here to write this trip down and he can look at bike parts to his hearts content. I feel like I have pulled an all-nighter. While I am looking for Lin, I find a large cup of coffee for a kick start. Lin isn't too hard to spot, with his long blonde tail under a bright red baseball hat. He is so predictable! He hasn't even made it through the first row yet.

I am so engrossed in writing down who, what, and how fucking amazing my journey was that I don't even hear Lin walk up behind me. He makes me jump by planting a kiss on my neck. He is pulling his little red wagon behind him. It is full of what makes him happy. Speaking of full, my journal is almost out of blank pages.

"Ok Mol, you have had your nose in that journal for weeks now. What ya working on?" Lin asks.

"I have been making notes and observations for the book I am going to write after I quit my job."

He looks a little surprised and asks "Are you serious Molly?"

"I was going to bring it up on the way home. I'm glad to hear you say that because I'm supposed to give the man my answer this week. When I talked to them yesterday, they said there's enough work to keep me busy for at least the next two years. They are talking about projects all over the world here, Mol." He continues "If you are really serious I think we need to get the house on the market and start making our plans since they're gonna want me to start right away. Now that the kids aren't buying the house we can make more money off of it and pay off any bills. We can start with a clear slate. Are you abso-fucking-lutely sure this is what you want to do?"

The only response I can come up with is "You have no idea how sure I am. I want to have time to write my book and take care of you. I have some things I need to tend to but I'll give the guys my notice this week. I should give them at least a month to find my replacement and time to train the new person. I can't just leave them high and dry, they have been too good to me. To us."

I can tell that Lin is all excited now. He has that sparkle in his eyes that I love. "Molly, this is gonna be a fantastic journey! Just you and me! I fucking love it! Give me an hour here, I'm supposed to talk to a man about some parts, then we can go home and call the kids" he says.

I get a huge smile (God, I love that smile) and a kiss that comes straight from his heart. Off he goes with a little spring in his step, pulling his wagon. He is so damn cute! How did I get so lucky?

It is time for me to make my list of what I have learned on this last adventure. I don't think I have left any of the memories out. I have filled up at least a dozen pages. I hope no one ever reads this journal, they would think I am bat-shit crazy or I have lapsed back into my teenage years taking acid. On second thought, fuck'em! It's my story I will write it like I want to! Those who know me can picture me now with my tongue sticking out. Ha-ha! I crack myself up sometimes! Back on task, I need to make a plan so this life change is as easy as possible:

1. I can make a trip within a trip. I just have to prepare in advance, or do I? What if I see a picture during one of my trips? Can I go off of that? It seems logical that I could. Another theory to test.

2. Things can travel back with me if I carry them, but for things to come into the present they have to be touching my skin. The flower did not come back but, the stains on my dress from the

Kennedy funeral did. I wonder what makes the difference. The stains were all me. I will have to test a stain made from an outside source.

3. If I can sell my "Janis" paper and pay off the house then when we sell it we get to keep all of the proceeds. How do I do this without lying to Lin? Before I worry about that, I need to find out what the value is. Do I have to sell all three pieces?

4. I need to visit Dmitri again and find out what can be seen when I pick things up or move objects. I already know I can bump into people and they can feel me. (Sorry, Joe).

5. I need to get the house ready to sell. Lots of cleaning, painting and over 20 years worth of life to box up. I love my house, but sometimes it haunts me. I am ready for new memories.

The ride home is full of excitement and plans. I think Lin is so amped about our new adventure that he forgets to tell me all about the parts he bought today. That's okay, it usually goes right over my head anyway. I don't need to know the difference between a fuel injector and a piston.

The next few months are going to be busier than a two-pecker Billy goat. Lin is going to get started on his new job and I am going to take care of business on this end. Once the house is sold, and Henry is settled where he needs to be, I can join Lin where ever he may be. I don't like it when we are apart, but we have to do this to make our plan work. I also want to make sure Allen and Henry are safe and sound before I go off to God-knows-where. I won't be working, so I can come back to Indiana as much as I want to. This may be often, since I will have a grandbaby to love and spoil! It is going to be hard to be away from the boys, but they will be stronger for it. It is time for them to make their own lives. Lin went to Georgia when he was 18. Tim moved in with me when we were still 18. It was a blast burning up ya-yas and learning along the way. Damn we had a good time!

Here it is Sunday morning again and we are back in the garage. Lin is putting the finishing touches on the '52. He is going to sell it so we can buy a camper to live in while we are on the road. I am not going to travel today. I have a lot on my plate for the week so enjoying this calm before the storm with Lin is my only plan. I have decided to write Dmitri a letter that I can give him rather then doing the mirror trick. I also found a picture of the shop and Dmitri dated 1964. I am going to use it. Hopefully, he has learned a few things about the charm that he can share with me.

Dear Dmitri,

   I hope you found the last envelope I left you. I'm sorry I didn't stick around to visit but I was on a mission and I was testing a theory. I have a few questions for you, please. You are the only person I can ask:

1. What do others see when I pick up objects?

2. Have you ever tried to communicate with someone during your travels?

3. What is the longest trip you have made?

4. What do you tell Anna? Where does she think you get all of this stuff? Does she know the truth?

5. Is there a place you have traveled to that caused you problems or danger? Have you ever been physically hurt?

I have learned that you can prepare for your journey and take items with you if you carry them on your person. I put a flower in my shoulder bag, but it did not travel back to the present with me. Because it was not touching my skin. I discovered it is possible to take a trip within a trip. I don't have much in the way of new information. I have made just one trip since the last time we talked. I know for you it has been 11 years, but for me it has only been a few days.

If you want a good time keep the weekend of June 16-18, 1967 open, and travel to Monterey California. If you like rock and roll music, you will love it! If you don't like the hippie culture, don't go. If that is the case, I think you should open up your mind and check it out. Those long-haired hippie freaks might just teach you something about humanity. If you want to have a really good time "inhale", you won't regret it.

That is all I can think of right now. Anything that you can share with me would be greatly appreciated. Do you have anything you want to ask me?

Your partner in time,

Molly

The drive to work on Monday morning goes by in a flash. I am nervous about telling Eric and Michael my plans. They have invested a lot of time into me, but I will help them get to life after Molly. I don't think there will be a problem finding someone who can do what I do. It is just my luck they are both in the office today. They have had their morning coffee so, let's get this done before

Eric leaves to fly a client to St. Louis. I finally get them both into Michael's office and without any fanfare or drama I just say "I am tendering my resignation". There are a few seconds of silence before Eric says "I called that one."

I don't have to tell them my plans, but I do. These guys have been my friends for the last seven years. Eric has always been straight up with me so he deserves the same respect. We decide to keep it on the down-low until a replacement is found. We have as much time as it takes to do this right.

Lin and I spend most of the week catching up with our kids. One by one, we tell them of our plans and that they are now set in motion. I come away feeling pretty good. I don't want Allen and Henry to feel like I am abandoning them, yet neither one of them even considered the notion. All four kids want us to be happy, bottom line. Thomas makes sure we both know we aren't spring chickens and we had better strike while the iron is hot! He says something to the humorous effect of "do it while you can still move around and you aren't pissing yourselves yet". Bless his heart.

Here it is Saturday morning and I am ready to get started towards a new direction. Lin just left to meet his new boss, Tom. I have the whole day to myself. So I have made arrangements with an appraiser to discuss my Monterey goodies. Obviously, I am going to make a road trip out of it. I don't want to sell this stuff close to home or use my real name. All of this dishonesty is driving me crazy. I am not going to do this again. In the future, I will make a dollar from writing a book about my observations. The only thing that sucks about that is it will be in the "fiction" section. I guess that is better than saying 'Hey, look at me! I can travel back in time'. (Watch me Mommy, watch me.)

When I walk in I see a man with a jewelers loop attached to his face. If he had a display screen across his forehead it would probably say "Oh, great, another piece of shit fake signature". I get the vibe that he is in a hurry to get me out of here so he can get on with his day.

I spread out my found booty on the counter for him to examine. After about twenty minutes of complete silence with a magnifying glass, Mr. Sam starts giggling like a school girl and doing a happy dance. He seems to very impressed with the signature page.

"Can I call a friend to come verify what I already know?" he asks.

After I give my consent, Sam lets me know it will be a wait. Evidently the dude is driving from Cleveland, and he won't be here for a couple of hours. I let him know," that's okay, I brought my laptop." I need to start planning my next trip any way. I settle into a corner and sit on the floor.

Now entering our forum is a (very serious looking) man named Jack. After brief introductions, he calmly opens his brief case and pulls out a large book. This must be a very important book, there is tissue paper sticking out from in between each page. Jack puts on white gloves and opens the book, very carefully turning each page. It reminds me of a hardcover scrapbook with removable borders. These hold the separated pieces of paper in place. Each piece blessed with a notable signature. He finds his desired page and Sam hands him my found doodle. Another period of silence begins. At least Jack grunts, and we get two "Hmmmm's." I don't see any emotion. He has a much better poker face than Sam does.

Jack lets Sam and I know that it is in fact a genuine Janis Joplin signature. A little voice in my head wants to say "No shit, Sherlock" but I have to be a good girl. After the boys whisper to each other a couple more times, they offer me $15,000 for all three pieces. You can't blame them for trying to low-ball me, it is their job. Bastards. I think the autograph alone is worth at least $20,000.

After we banter back and forth a few times. I accept $27,000 for all of it. My only stipulation is…cash, please. They let me know that they have just enough time to get to the bank if I am willing to wait. I watch Jack walk to his car. Once he gets outside, the stoic facade falls off and he does a little happy-boy jig. This is cool! I have made two men very happy, enough money to take a chunk out of the mortgage, and I didn't steal. I decide to put 20K towards the bank note and keep the rest to buy paint and whatever else I may need to get the house ready to sell. I am not going to say anything to Lin right now. If it becomes an issue later, I will deal with it then.

Getting back home I have decided to go visit Dmitri. I want to get my questions answered before making a destination decision. All the doors are locked and I have what is needed to get me to where I want to go. As far as I know, Dmitri and I are in a

Chapter Twelve

League of our own.

Dmitri is walking a photographer to the door. Time has been kind to him. Where is Anna? I don't think Dmitri is into the hippie "free love" scene, his hair is very short and he is wearing creased pants with a cardigan sweater. He is very handsome, but he reminds me of Mr. Rogers. I hear little feet coming down the stairs. A sweet looking little girl jumps the last three steps with a pop and a giggle. By the way she is dressed, I am guessing she is off to school for the day. Dmitri says "Ah, my little Pani". The angel-face giggles out a reply "I am not a Lady Poppa. I am a girl. I am only seven." He gives her a laughing kiss on the cheek and out the door she goes to feed her brain.

As he is putting the money into the register, I lay my note down on the display case. What a cool customer. He doesn't even stop counting and says "Hello, where have you been my friend? Get into da mirror over dere so I can see you." He opens my letter and starts answering my questions one by one.

"I did not realize da answer to your first question until da last time you visited me. When you picked up da pen to write on your hand, da pen disappeared while you were touching it. Once it left your hand it became visible to me on dis side of da mirror."

"I have not tried to make myself known when I travel" he continues. "I like to get in and get out. Aldough I have spent some time walking around Queen Victoria's Buckingham Palace. What a beautiful place, so full of antiques! I do not take anyting from famous places. If I did, I would have a few of da crown jewels. I do most of my shopping in antique shops or street markets.

"Anna never knew how I get dese treasures" he explains. "I lost my beloved wife when our daughter was born so now it is just da two of us.

Da only time I have come close to harm was when an angry dog could smell me. Beware of da animals, dey can sense you."

"Dis Monterey thing? I like some of da songs I hear on da radio but I prefer classical. I will keep da date in my mind. Have you tried to travel to a time using just a mental image?" he asks.

I reach into my trusty bag to dig out a notebook. We are both startled by the bell ringing above the door. Dmitri gives me a wink and points to a little table in the corner. I make myself comfortable and silently observe Dmitri doing his thing. The couple that has joined us appears to be a middle-aged woman and her father. The man is wearing dark glasses. He is also carrying a white cane folded up and tucked under his arm. This makes me want to test a theory. I am blind in one eye since birth. I have some insight (no pun intended) into this test. My hearing is pretty incredible. Logic would say I should be half-deaf as loud as I like my music. If it's too loud you're too old!

I already know Dmitri can't hear me but do special circumstances warrant special rules? The gentleman with the cane waits patiently for his daughter. Dmitri is showing her a necklace. I start to hum Yankee Doodle Dandy with a side of percussion via a pen and pad of paper. The man instantly tilts his head up, and turns his face in my direction. It is very obvious that he does hear me. Interesting! I am being heard! He doesn't seem uncomfortable or afraid. For all he knows I am another customer in the store. Note to self, saying "fuck" around a blind nun is not a good idea. I finish up my note to Dmitri just as the couple is leaving. I hear the man whistling "Yankee Doodle" as he goes out the door, holding his daughters arm.

Dmitri picks up my note and walks over to the mirror behind the counter. I like watching his facial reactions as he reads.

Hello my Friend,

Thank you for the information on picking up objects. This is good to know and I bet it makes your adventures easier. We've learned an important fact together.

I'm sorry to know about Anna. She seemed like a lovely woman. Your daughter is absolutely adorable and she acts very smart. She is so full of energy and life.

Amazing! I just learned that the blind gentleman could hear me. I hummed a tune and he turned his head towards me as I was doing it. Then he was whistling it as he went out the door.

What do you mean travel with "mental images"? Do you mean without a picture? The first time I traveled, I came back here after the shop was closed. I didn't have a physical picture and it wasn't planned. I didn't even know this ability existed. I do know I was thinking about you and the shop when I touched the charm. Please explain….

Molly

Dmitri looks at me through the mirror and says "I like your new discovery. I had an odd experience wit a blind beggar once and now it makes sense. I will see my Anna again. Right now my purpose is to raise our daughter to be a good, healty and happy woman."

"When I say mental image, it is more a question of imagination. When you traveled back here you had a point of reference because you had been here. Write down a date or a specific point in time you would like to visit. Before you touch da charm, let your imagination take you dere. Accuracy doesn't really matter, but keep da picture in your mind simple and uncluttered."

I write down "Washington DC August 1864" and envision a warm summer day at the Custis-Lee Mansion. I'm not real good with pure imagination. Fake chitty-chatter pleasantries are a waste of time, and I am on a mission. I blow Dmitri a kiss and wave goodbye before I touch the charm. Batta-bing-batta-boom, I am standing in front of the Custis-Lee mansion again.

What I see is not what I expect at all. I am surrounded by Union soldiers and, unfortunately, my sense of smell isn't on the fritz right now. Wow! Some of these guys really need a bath and a toothbrush. I do not see thousands of graves, only a few in the distance. I walk around the grounds and notice the groomed flower gardens around the mansion. In a rose garden are at least 20 new graves. Who in the world would put them so close to the house when there are acres of property below the hill. How ironic is it that this was once the home of George Washington's great grand son-in-law, none other than Robert E. Lee himself? Now the enemy is using it as a Headquarters. I don't think either of the Georges' (the father of our country or his grandson) would appreciate the irony.

I also notice there are many colored people around the mansion. They seem to be taking care of business and chores. Watching the human interaction, I don't get the feeling of forced labor. But men always have pecking order, especially in the military. The phrase "organized chaos" comes to mind.

The only women I see are carrying baskets of vegetables to the separate kitchen building. They are all dressed in the same long dresses with do-rags covering their hair. The women are black *and* white. The girls are all laughing and chattering away while they work together to reach a common goal. I personally don't like sharing my kitchen, but this doesn't seem to be the case here. My guess is these ladies feed all of the officers but not the enlisted men. No woman in her right mind would let a man that smells as bad as some of these guys sit at her dinner table.

I see a wagon loaded with crates of fresh vegetables and I overhear the driver say he is going to the White House. The tone of his voice tells me he is not thrilled about the trip, something to the effect of "I hate that damned Long Bridge". I notice a long empty bench right behind the driver's seat. This is a no-brainer! I hop into the wagon to avoid a long walk. As we are pulling away, I hear someone shout "Don't forget to pick up the wine barrels and sugar." My chauffer throws up his arm in response and mumbles under his breath, "Now I'm a damn errand boy! This will cost them a few pints of ale."

I am astonished at how everything looks so different. Many years from now this area is lined with white tombstones, but today it is just land, many trees and union soldiers. There are tents and men everywhere. It is probably a good thing that there are so many camp fires going or this place would smell like a cloud of bad body odor! I see ruffled men taking a minute to rest before they head back into battle. Some of the soldiers are gathered around fires calmly trading stories. I also notice, the occasional lonely soul with his back propped up against a tree. Some staring blankly into space while others are writing letters or napping. Unlike the atmosphere at the mansion, these men all seem abnormally somber.

Oh wow! There is Freedman's Village. All of the homes are the same, lined up in dirty little rows. The first boring housing addition with HOA (home owner association) fees, literally. What a sad place. Thousands of people run away from enforced labor in the south to a broken society. I think maybe the intentions are good by offering work, education and healthcare for all who dare to venture north. The idea is a fairy tale that in reality is a military enforced segregation and slavery. Many "people of color" work the gardens and fields growing food for the union troops. They aren't allowed to partake in the fruits of their labor and have to pay to live in the cracker box houses. Hunger and unhealthy living conditions are not part of the "Freedom Dream". This is not a sight of a promised land. What a horrifying way to see your dreams get crushed. The north is no more prepared for the changes than the south. This time the "Massa" is the United States government enforced by the United States Armed Forces. I don't think this is what Abe has in mind, although he is a fan of segregation. He agrees the races are different and should live separated, but work together as humans. Some families leave slavery and make a better life for themselves. Others, not so much.

What a relief, we are finally past the populated areas. My senses need a break! Imagine a line of full "Port-a-Potties" on a hot August day. I do want some fresh air please. The country side is absolutely beautiful. Everything is so green and the birds are singing. It is all very peaceful. So sad that all of these gorgeous trees will be cleared to make a city. How much wilderness has been destroyed because of ego and population growth? Such a shame all humans don't adhere to the keep it simple stupid (K.I.S.S.) philosophy. We pass an occasional wagon on the road. Mr. Personality grunts out a "Howdy" and keeps on heading down the road. I bet he would have a better outlook if he washed his gross uniform, shaved, and cuddled up to a bar of soap.

We make it to the bridge, which is crawling with soldiers and people. We have to wait in a line of wagons and buggies. It is a traffic jam! I don't see tail lights, anyone flipping the bird or hear any horns. The atmosphere still feels the same. There is a soldier standing at the entrance of the bridge that keeps yelling "Keep it mov'in folks."

As we cross, it all becomes very serious with hints of road rage from the horses. I don't hear or see anyone being rude. Everyone is just getting to where they need to go. I hope our horse is having a good day despite the jackass driving. I have yet to hear anything positive come out of his mouth. In fact I think he is a grouch who doesn't care where he spits his nasty tobacco juice. Case and point: He is making it sport to see how many passing horses he can hit with his disgusting spit. Most of the men tip their hat when they pass a wagon carrying a lady, not this grump ass. I am kicking him to the curb as soon as we get across this river. If he bitches this much to himself, I want no part of him when he is among other human beings, especially after he starts drinking.

Ok I feel like Astronaut Taylor/Charlton Heston when he is looking at the Statue of Liberty in the movie Planet of the Apes. There is the Washington Memorial. It is unfinished and short. It doesn't look like a work in progress. I don't see any humans, but I'll be damned if there aren't cows grazing all around the monument. As I walk amongst the cows, I notice they do sense me and move out of the way as I get close to them. I lean up against the monument for a smoke and look out. Let me tell you what I don't see. There is no reflecting pool, no mall, no walls or statues. The most shocking thing is no Lincoln Memorial. The land looks swampy (and smells stinky) and the Potomac is right there on the other side of the soggy, nasty-looking ground. How in the piss do you move a river and get rid of a swamp? Why in the hell would you pick this awful land as a place to build tributes to our fallen heroes? I can tell I am in the city, but it is far from the metropolis it will become. As far as the other monuments go the events leading to their conception hasn't even happened yet. It is almost a burden to know how history plays out. Here and now the focus is a war between the states, a deadly quarrel between siblings. The ugliness of a true enemy is a distant memory. The fight with England does not even compare to the cruelty of the battles yet to come, when the British will be our ally.

  I keep thinking of my Dad, and his adventure in this city while he was in the Army. He was 17 years old when he asked Granny to sign the papers for him to enlist. It is hard for me to believe he was younger then Henry is now. I think I might be feeling a little bit of the same wonderment and awe he felt. Dad never stepped off the beautiful hills of Kentucky until he joined the service. My culture shock is, I know of the yet to come as well as the history of the here and now. It is a good thing I wore comfy shoes, because I am going to soak in as much history as I can.

  The Smithsonian is an amazing building. It looks more like a big elaborate brick church than an institute. There are many "suits" walking around. Speaking of suits, I must have passed where the Pentagon will be. Damn, I wasn't paying attention and I missed it. I also notice there aren't any women going into the Smithsonian. I am glad to know that society's expectation of women to remain uneducated and unworthy of opinion will be remedied. I think there is a definite difference between men and women but just because you piss standing up doesn't make you any smarter. As a mother of two boys, cleaning the floor around the toilet is proof of it.

As I walk along the streets, I notice how life is very simple, yet hard for some. Looking around at the different faces, I can definitely distinguish those who work for a living from the high society people who don't. The fancy women are holding handkerchiefs up to their noses to guard against the smell. Give me a fucking break! I bet they don't fart or burp either.

A large posting board appears to be a gathering point. As I get closer I can see this is where the dead, missing and deserter lists are published. Education has come a long way. I notice children reading the lists for their moms who cannot read. It is a heart-breaking sight. To think, when my boys were this age they were concerned about their current baseball position, not hoping their dad's name wasn't on a list.

There are many soldiers marching in formation through the streets. Some of these poor guys just look beat to hell and tired, all the way down to their bones. I see more than a few uniformed men using crutches because of an injury or they have a sleeve pinned up due to a missing arm. Some things never change. The older men look like they have peered into the gates of hell and the youngsters are full of themselves, talking about how much "Johnny Reb" ass they are going to kick. I see civilian men, but they are dressed as businessmen, in suits. The few farmers I see have obvious reasons why they are not fighting. They are either too young, too old, or physically maimed.

Sweet! There is a horse drawn street car that is almost empty. Since it isn't moving real fast, jumping on is no problem. Lying on the floor is a "Harpers Weekly" magazine. I maneuver into position and pick it up when no one is looking. I love the fact that I can look over my treasure now instead of later. "General Grant's Campaign" is the story of the week. It is about the crossing of the James River on July 26, 1864. The images are drawings, not photographs. It is still in pretty good shape, so I put it in my bag as a gift for Dmitri. The car is getting too full for my taste; it is hard to stay out of the way without getting stepped on. Looking at the sun in the sky, I am guessing it to be around 6:00 pm. I'm back to walking.

I decide to check out the Willard Hotel, such a magnificent building. I think I hit the dinner hour, big mistake on my part. I don't want to explore bad enough to mingle through that many people. Next is the Treasury Building, which is still under construction.

There is the White House. I walk right up the semi-circle drive under the portico. The horse carriages are pulling up to the steps from Pennsylvania Avenue. There is a statue of Thomas Jefferson holding the Declaration of Independence in the middle of a circle garden. I think poor Tom needs some attention, he is all green and moldy. There is a wrought iron fence on both sides of the driveway. I do not see the large famous chandelier lighting the doorway, but multiple gaslights. There are many people walking around. I see men in little groups, having bullshit sessions (if they were women they would be having "bitchfests") all around me.

As I cross the threshold, I am hit in the face with an afternoon heat that has been bottled up all day. There are two men very gently moving the crowd towards the door, then outside. Bob and weave, Molly, bob and weave. Once I get past the moving mass of bodies, exploring is easy. There must be a social function tonight. There are busy bees coming out of the woodwork. There is even a band setting up in the corner. This is the first time I have ever been inside the White House. It is very beautiful, but not what I expect. It smells like a hot, old cigar. There are numerous old paintings of previous presidents and large mirrors adorning the walls. I walk between a set of large white pillars and find myself in a long corridor. I look right and see a grand stair case. I exit stage left.

I enter a very large room. It is really tacky by decorating standards of the present. The carpet is a red and blue floral pattern, like something you would see in a hotel, not a home. There is a massive glass chandelier hanging from the ceiling in the middle of the room. Again with the big ass mirrors! I don't know anyone who likes looking at themselves this much.

I see two women standing by a window. The short, round woman is not very happy and is loudly making it known. As I get closer, I realize it is Mary Todd Lincoln. She is holding out the draperies and showing another woman where a large piece has been cut out of the cloth. "These drapes are new and now they are ruined because someone has been allowed to stand here and cut into them. I am to be held accountable to Mr. Lincoln for every penny I spend on this house. I do not understand people coming into my home seeking souveniers at my expense. I will not stand for it!"

The other woman just keeps nodding her head in agreement. My guess is that this is the only response you can give the first lady without receiving her wrath. Mrs. Lincoln stomps off, saying "I will be discussing this with the President."

There you have it ladies and gentleman; a spoiled brat tantrum at its finest! The poor girl she was venting to is examining the curtains as if she is trying to figure out a way to fix them. I think I have seen enough. There is nothing here that tweaks my history loving-fascination. It is just a room that is too big, gaudy and void of personality.

There is an amazing half-moon window halfway up the stairs. It is a landing, and you have to make a turn to continue to the second floor. At the top there is another long hallway lined with chairs and benches. Peeking through the doors I can see bedrooms. Looking in the room to my right, I notice a cluttered desk, a huge headboard on a large bed, and a really cool marble-topped table. My guess is that this room belongs to Abe. It smells like a man's room. The papers on the desk look like unfinished speeches or ideas. Looking at the lines crossed out and the chicken scratches, they are not final drafts. I don't see anything that has his signature on it. Here is one that has a date of May, 24 1864 written in the corner. The heading is one word "Dream". It is obvious that this beautiful, troubled mind is recording his dreams. How corny is it that one hundred years from now a colored man, fighting the same fight in a different way, will give a very famous speech about having a dream? Now this is the kind of shit that gives me goose bump body chills. How fucking lucky am I to be here?

   The rest of the floor consists of bedrooms and a couple of offices at the other end of the hallway.   This house just does not feel like a home. It feels more like an office building with sleeping quarters. Believe it or not, the most interesting room in the whole house is the kitchen in the basement. I see that "Mr. Personality", my driver has made his delivery. There is a lot of activity going on here and it smells incredible! I have been walking around the White House for at least three hours. I have yet to see the President and I am getting hungry looking at all of this food. They won't miss a carrot. I wander back to the main entrance stopping along the way to listen in on private conversations. It is a good thing I don't have to be quiet, just explore and munch. I must have missed the highlight of the party. The music still plays on, but a few people are leaving. If the Lincolns are still here why would anyone leave the party? It is time for me to go back outside. I think the last part of this journey is going to be a walk to the Lincoln's "summer house".

It is a beautiful evening, so I hoof it. The heat of the day is gone and as soon as I get out of the stuffy city my walk becomes very relaxing. I hear the night critters, and after being around stinky people all day the air is a welcomed relief for my nose. This is a perfect place to slow my roll. It isn't pitch black out because there is a nice bright moon. I have my pen light in my bag, but I like the peaceful solitude of the night. Sometimes, I crave quiet and I don't mind being by myself.

I hear hoofs walking down the road, coming towards me. The rider isn't in a big hurry. Evidently, they are enjoying the peaceful night themselves. Unless my eyes are fooling me, I see a tall stove-pipe top hat. Are you fucking kidding me? As he gets closer, I can see that it is, in fact Abraham Lincoln. Suddenly the horse rears up and I hear a gun shot. In one split second I am amazed that I am looking at Abe, then I am getting out of the way of a freaked-out horse that takes off running without his rider. I jump right into a briar bush. I feel the thorns all over my body. Considering I am not wearing much, I am screwed.

Once I finally get untangled, I notice Abe is lying on the road and he is not moving. I take out my pen light and slowly walk up to him. He has been shot in the head. I am

100% sure he is no longer living. He is giving me the "dead man stare". Oh fuck! Oh fuck! OH FUCK! I spooked the horse and now history has been changed. I hear multiple horses heading this way coming from the direction that Abe was traveling. They are moving fast! I hurry and stash my light. It is time for me to leave. I will have to come back and fix this. I really hope it works that way. Will a few months really

Chapter Thirteen

Make that much of a difference?

I am home and covered in cuts. I look at my body and see blood everywhere. The thorns are sticking in my skin and clothes. Thank God my glasses protected my eyes because my face didn't escape injury. Think about this for one fucking minute Molly! You can obviously get hurt on your travels. I am amping up to a real freak out moment here. What if I get hurt and I can't get back home? What if I die? Am I playing with the shear existence of Henry and Allen? What happens to my present if I die in the past? If I die before I am born, do I get a redo by being born as scheduled or what? Oh my God….what the fuck am I doing? It's all fun and games until someone loses a fucking eye.

Before I move into complete wig-out mode, Henry walks in. Pull it back Molly, don't let him see you lose it.

"Hey Mom, why are all the doors locked? Oh wow! What the hell happened to you? You're bleeding and crying. Are you ok?" he asks.

I just blow off the questions by saying I got into a fight with a berry bush and it won. He sits down and I can tell something has been working on him and he needs to talk.

"Can you call me into school on Monday, he asks. I don't want to go and be a part of what I know is gonna happen. I don't understand the ugliness and I don't feel that way."

I have no clue what he is talking about and ask him to tell me the whole story. He gives me a look like I have three heads.

"Where have you been, Mom? They're busing in black kids on Monday. The county closed two schools so now they're coming to Central Noble. Didn't you see it in the paper? I heard the ladies in the office say that Governor Zachary is sending the Indiana Guard to make sure everything is peaceful. Some of the kids are planning a boycott and are gonna refuse to go to class. I'm not afraid, I just don't get the logic. I'm not the only one. The whole baseball team feels this way. We are kind of excited about a couple boys who will be on those buses. There's one guy I've seen pitch and I'm tellin' ya no one can hit his curve ball and I hear he has a killer batting average", he explains.

He continues to plead his case "Coach Deter isn't sure if the school is gonna let them be on the team or not. So if I make a stand it will be if they aren't allowed to play not right now. I don't care if they bus in purple people with green polka dots if one of them has a good arm or can swing a stick."

I am thinking to myself, what the fuck just happened? I agree to call in his absence as a stall tactic until I can figure this out. That seems to be what he wants to hear, so off he goes, doing what eighteen-year-old boys do. My guess is he is texting the baseball team.

I hear a shower calling my name. I need to wash this blood off, pick out the thorns and clear my head to figure out a way to fix this.

Amazing what a warm shower and a cold beer can do to calm emotions. I turn on the news and am definitely not in Kansas anymore, so to speak. I keep expecting Rod Serling to pop out and tell me I have entered "The Twilight Zone". As I flip through the channels I notice there are no colored people on TV. I mean zero, all of the commercials, all of the talk shows, all of the sports channels, and all of the music channels have not one person of color. I flip to C-Span, and I am completely shocked to see a Confederate flag standing along side the American flag in Congress. I do not see any women or colored people on the floor of Congress. Hold the phone Ethel! What the fuck is going on here? It is like the civil rights movement has been postponed 50 years. Does this change have anything to do with my trip?

My research tells me that Lincoln died instantly in August 1864 of a fatal gun shot wound while traveling to the summer cottage. Vice President Hannibal Hamlin took over the Presidency. A weak, unthinking man by any standard. The south saw this as an opportunity and captured the White House. Jefferson Davis became President of the United States after the coup de ta. Davis served in this position until his death in 1889. Then his son-in-law, Joel Addison Hayes Jr., took over the position until 1919, when he died. The United States became a slave nation when the civil war ended abruptly due to the take-over.

The news channels on TV are running segments about a small group in Rhode Island, trying to take the rebel flag out of all government buildings and schools. The commentary tells me they're fighting a losing battle. The Thirteenth Amendment pertains to charging taxes. Slavery isn't abolished until the Twenty Third Amendment in 1947.

Holt shit, what have I done? The mistake I made is affecting the life of my son. The whole United States has changed, but bringing it into Henry's life hurts me to my core. I have got to fix this. The civil rights movement is a very large, ugly part of history. I am sorry so many people had to go through this narrow-minded part of life, but I am going to be selfish and not let it touch my children. Racism is an ugly hatred in its purest form, real or unjust. Too many people falsely play that card when it benefits them, lines their pockets or covers up a truth. There are two kinds of people in my world, ass-hole and non ass-hole no matter the color, period. Content of character, plain and simple.

If I go back to a time before meeting Abe on that dark road, can I change the outcome? It has been documented that a shot missed Lincoln and put a hole through his hat. Common sense tells me that since I spooked the horse and it reared up, the bullet found flesh. How in the hell did I happen to go back on *that* night? Coincidence or not, at the end of the day, a powerful lesson has been learned. I could just say that it figures and it is just my luck, but it doesn't change the fact that now I have to fix it. To my favor, I can pull a strong point of reference from my memory.

I need to make a plan for my trip. I was in such an all-fired hurry I didn't take the magazine out of my bag. I left the treasure I wanted to give Dmitri in 1864. I will have to see if I can find something to replace it. That shouldn't be real hard, considering my goal is to do nothing. No walking to Lincoln's Summer House. (Go the opposite direction, Molly. "Stay off the moors",ha ha.) I am brought out of my own little deep thought of humor by a knock on the door. It is our good buddy, Benedict.

Talk about a history buff. Benedict enjoys researching the past just as much as I do. We always get into a good conversation. Lin should be home soon and I obviously have forgotten that we invited Benedict and Ann over for a few beers with some burgers on the grill. I want to correct my error as soon as possible, but maybe I can learn something in this changed present about the altered past. Benedict is a Civil War enthusiast and has done a lot of reading about the subject and era. I mean think about it, no Martin Luther King Jr. or Rosa Parks? Were these famous civil right figures once slaves? Are the lunch counter "sit-ins" going on right now? Do the Freedom Riders still make a stand, or is that something that hasn't happened yet? This is shit I have to find out. I know I have changed the present but what about the history I grew up reading about? My trip will have to wait until I answer a few of these odd silent questions.

Lin is a master with a grill. There must be something to the notion of "man with fire equals good food". Staying true to form with full bellies, we get into a deep round table after I tell them about Henry's request for school on Monday. We all agree that times have got to change and racism is an ugly evil. I decide to throw it out there and see where it sticks and ask "what do you think would have happened to this country if Abraham Lincoln would have lived"?

Benedict gets a serious look on his face and says "The north had the war all but won and finished. All that was left was for Lee to surrender to Grant. Indiana and the rest of the union nation would never have been brought into slavery. I also think he would have ended one man owning another man based on the color of his skin all over the nation. Slavery as a culture did not begin with the blacks. Let's not forget about indentured servants. The only difference is choice."

Ann says, "Did you hear about that black woman in Chicago who refused to move to the back of the bus when a white woman wanted her seat? I heard on the news that the police knocked her out and pulled her off the bus by her feet."

I am shocked by Lin's response, "That is what happens in big cities. At least here in our small town we can keep the peace by living with each other, black and white, if we all go home to our parts of town every night. I agree it isn't right, but if that keeps narrow-minded people from fighting, then so be it".

Benedict responds "Lin, your parents were fed by black wet nurses just like mine. We are all products of white men raping or loving black women. We all have a mixture somewhere in our family tree. Why is it so difficult for all of us to live with each other on a human level without classes based on color? "

I must be sitting here with my mouth hanging open, because I have a very bad case of cotton mouth and Lin is giving me a funny look.

Okay, this is crazy. Not only has it touched my child, but Lin and my friends have a whole new perspective that I don't like. To them this is normal every day life and thoughts. They don't like the line being drawn in the sand, but they are ignorant and unwilling to change the times or make a stand against status quo. After Benedict and Ann leave and the kitchen gets cleaned up, Lin and I tuck ourselves in bed with a good movie. Lin doesn't notice that I have my trusty travel bag around my neck, under my sleeping t-shirt. This is the first time I have traveled with Lin lying next to me. Since I close my eyes, he will think I have fallen asleep. I really

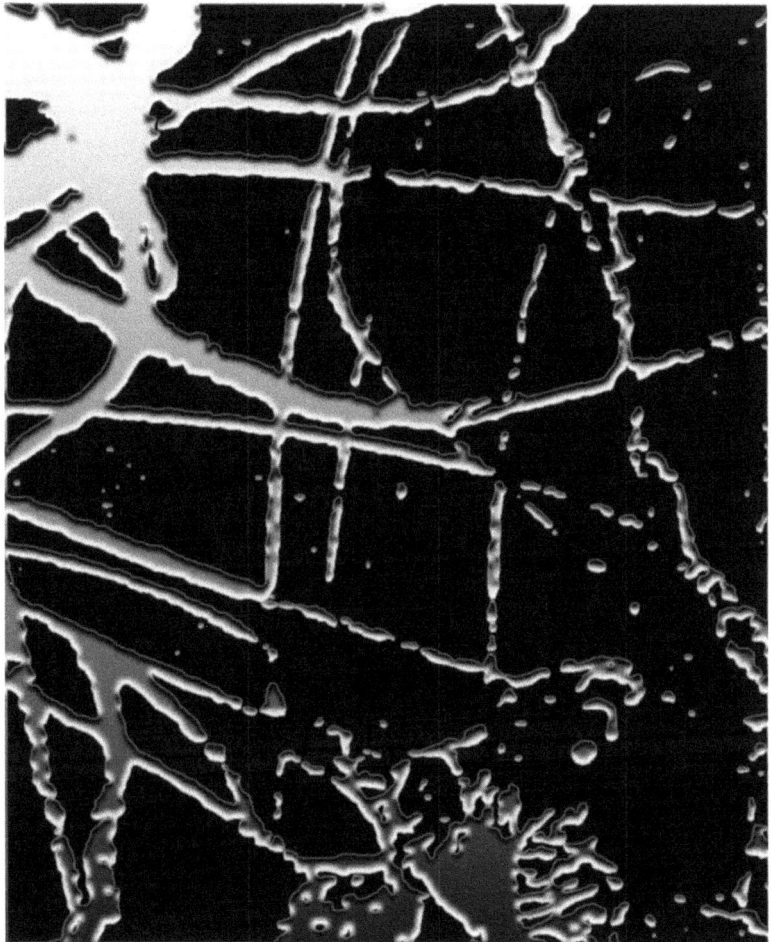

Chapter Fourteen

Need to fix my mistake.

I have picked my point of reference to be the small boy from my last trip. His image is burned in my memory. He is one of the children reading the posted soldier reports. He reminded me of Allen with his big blue eyes and dirty blonde hair. I would say he is about eleven years old. His mother is standing next to him as he looks over the names. The scene is all very familiar. I hear many woman saying "Praise the Lord" full of joy, and I see many broken hearts. The small boy says "Mama he isn't here. President Hamlin has spared him again." His mother buries her face in the blanket wrapped around the baby she is carrying, and weeps.

Now wait a pea picking minute here, President Hamlin? What the fuck? How in the piss did I get here? Same boy; same place; same scene; different time. This isn't going to be as easy as I thought. Think Molly. Pick a memory that is specific to that day. I don't remember reading the exact date on anything. I realize this poor child must have looked at these lists more often then I care to think about. Every time the same fear and dread going in. Twice I have seen the relief on his face to know his father might be coming home soon. I wonder what happens to them in the end. I can't research this when I get home because I do not know his name. The irony of this is that if his father's name would have been listed, then I wouldn't have to look it up later because I would know what happened. I would rather not know his name.

The thought of the kitchen and my stolen carrot might work. I touch the charm and I feel the instant warmth of the large fires burning, and the smell of good food. This feels like de ja vue. All of the faces look familiar and everyone seems to be in the right spot, including the carrots. I decide to forego the munchie this time and make a mad dash to the main entrance. This is no easy task. Have you ever tried to dodge those big-ass dresses? There are many people milling around. The dynamics seem to stand the test of time; women with their heads together gossiping; men talking about how, if they were in charge, they could fix the worlds' problems. Young couples are walking arm in arm while flirting with each other.

Sure enough, I see Abraham Lincoln telling a man who appears to be a butler, "Mrs. Lincoln has retired upstairs with a headache and I am going to the summer cottage. Please be sure after the last guest is gone that you do your best to have everything cleaned up. That way Mrs.

Lincoln has nothing to yell about when I return in the morning. I bid you a goodnight."

He doesn't go out the front, door where a few men seem to be mindlessly waiting for him but instead walks towards me and the kitchen. Those long legs don't skip a beat, and I have to practically run to keep up. Abe dips his head to all of the ladies, but keeps on walking. His pace is impossible to stop, and everyone moves out of his way. He walks through the kitchen, praising the ladies for the wonderful meal, and right out the back door. As he puts on his hat, he calls over his shoulder, "You have not seen me."

I decide to hang out in the kitchen for a little while and listen to the ladies chatter as they finish cleaning up. They start to gossip about Abe and Mary sleeping in separate houses. They all agree that Mary probably complains in her sleep. There is a plump lady sitting on a chair, puffing on a corn cob pipe. She gives a big belly laugh and says "Separate bedrooms, separate buildings. I am surprised they have three sons. Honestly, could you live, much less sleep with that woman?"

Everyone laughs, until three men in uniforms walk in, demanding to know if they have seen the president. Silence takes over the room and no one moves. One of the soldiers walks over to the round woman, who is evidently in charge.

"Maggie, have you seen President Lincoln?" he asks.

Maggie gives her pipe a long draw and an even longer exhale. "Now John, if I have seen him why would I tell you? So that you can take away one of the few moments of peace the man has? Between Mrs. Lincoln, people wanting favors, and you soldiers crawling all over the place, how can the man catch a breath? So help me Hanna, the poor feller can't even go to the water closet without being bothered!"

After Maggie has spewed out what she thinks, she sits back in her chair and sucks on her pipe, just daring the soldier to poke any further. One of the other soldiers decides to defuse the situation and exclaims "John, you are wasting time! Obviously, he isn't here. Let's go upstairs and look. Charlie here will ride to the summer house now and get word back to us."

Logic takes over, and all three men leave. Damn, Maggie backed him right down and gave the President at least a ten minute head start.

I decide to hang out with John and this other dude. I won't be on the road to spook the horse, so I know Abe will make it, safe and sound. History will be corrected, or at least I won't be the one to fuck it up. Charlie does as he is told and takes off on a horse with two other men. John and Mr. Logical go upstairs to find the President's room empty. Neither one of them attempt to knock on Mary's door, but they stop in front of it. Just like a little boy, John says "you do it.' The other man responds "No, you do it, but do it lightly."

John looks at the door to get his courage up. Just as he is about to knock, the door opens and out walks a maid carrying dirty laundry. John asks her, "Is Mr. Lincoln in there?"

The maid looks to be about 13 years old. Very young and embarrassed by the question, she giggles covers her face, and says "No Sir." The men turn and walk away, leaving her there in a blush.

We all go back downstairs, which is now almost completely empty. I don't see any guests. I only see people cleaning up and moving furniture. The band is packed up and walking out the front door. I see a few young people hanging out in the corner. The girls look to be maids and the men are soldiers. They appear to be very respectful to each other, but they are flirting. Hormones are fully engaged. The girls giggle right on cue. Oh, to be that young again. On second thought, no thanks. John walks over and tells the kids to break it up (party pooper). He also orders one of the guys standing at attention to go outside and wait for a message from the summer house. Ok, now I have a new man to bird dog.

We wait outside for what seems like an eternity. This guy is boring to hang out with. So far I have seen him pick his nose and eyeball the girls as they come out of the White house. Finally, Charlie rides up and asks my horny nose-picking friend, "Where is Captain Stephens?"

They both go back inside and I quickly figure out John's last name. Charlie waits for the young nose-picker to get the hint that his services are no longer required before he exclaims "John, we have a problem. President Lincoln cannot sneak out by his self no more. By the grace of God, he was not killed tonight. Someone took a shot at him, but it missed and put a hole right through his hat. The men are combing the woods, but chances are we aren't going to find anything. The President is a good man, but a damned fool. He shrugged it off and went to bed as if noth'in happened".

This is what I needed to hear. Mission accomplished. This tape can self-destruct at any time, because the man still breaths. I have had enough of fixing, now I want to see if it really worked. Abe is safe even if it is

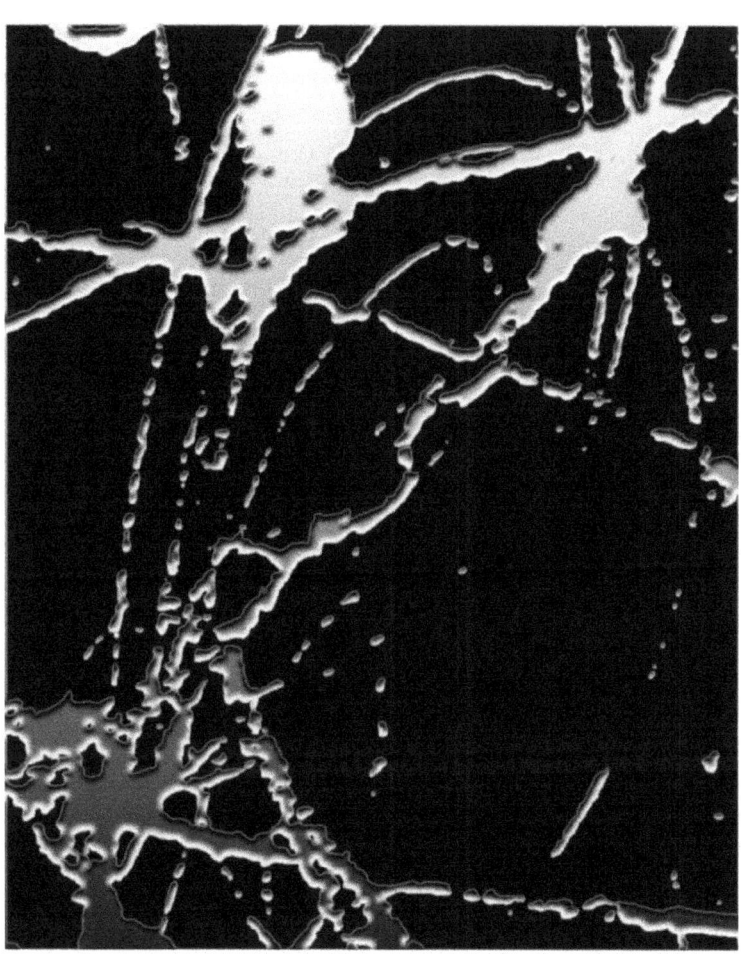

Chapter Fifteen

Only for a few months.

Lin is still watching the movie and everything looks the same. I didn't even look for anything to give to Dmitri. I will have to remedy this on my next trip. Quit saying it, Molly, and do it for shit's sake.

I get out of bed and take a stroll through the house. Nothing seems out of place and all is quiet on the home front. Henry is asleep in his room with our snoring dog that takes up the whole lower half of a full size bed. I turn on the television in the kitchen and I see a special on PBS about Jimi Hendrix. So far so good. I change the channel and there is a news clip showing President Obama boarding Air Force One. All seems as it should be. Dodged a bullet there, Molly. I guess I should say "Abe".

God I love Sunday mornings; slow start with coffee time. Lin tells me about his meeting with Tom yesterday. They want him to start working right away.

"Molly we need to get this house on the market and you need to get your job wrapped up" he explains. "Tom wants me to start a job in Houston. He said it will be about six months straight, working six-12's. We can make bank. The money we get from the house and this job will get us back to square zero. I told him about our plans and he is going to try to make this move for us as smooth as possible. He is working on a job for me after the Houston gig in South Bend. I can drive home every day and do what needs to be done to get this house sold. At least I can work on packing up the garage. I don't want you to deal with that. This can work, Molly. By that time Henry will be close to moving into the dorms at school. I hope Tom wasn't talking shit, but he said there is the possibility of a long job in the Bahamas starting next year. What a great place for you to start your book."

How fucking cool would it be to sit on a beach in real time and go wherever I want in travel "time". There is a lot of work to be done to reach this goal. We start making a list of things I can do to the house while Lin is in Houston. I have the feeling that the next year for Lin and I will be a busy one. There is nothing like trying to do it "all" in a matter of months. Let's see, a graduation from high school, right into the college scene, becoming a Granny, selling a house and being jobless, which hasn't happened since I was 14. Well, there were six months I had off while being paid severance. I worked for the same employer twenty years to get that. It still makes me sad to know that one man worked his whole life to make a very profitable company, only to have it sold and ripped apart after he died. That's not even taking into consideration all the shit I have to do with the house. Wow, Lord give me strength to keep my shit together.

We make our way to the garage so Lin can put the last finishing touches on the '52. He has a guy coming by around 4:00 to look at it. If he buys it, then we can add shopping for a camper to the long list of shit to do. Lin would like this to happen sooner than later. Once my man takes a notion there is no stopping him. My job is to figure out a way to make it all happen. He wants to pull the camper down to Houston so he can have a home base and we can save money. I decide to take this day as the "calm before the storm" and do research for my next trip. I have a feeling that my trips are going to have to be short and sweet for the next few months. After my last adventure, I need to go somewhere for fun. There are so many things I want to see. I get out my trusty journal and start making a list of where I do and don't want to go.

1. JFK shooting – I could watch Lee Harvey Oswald take that first shot and miss (in my opinion). See if the fatal wound actually came from a secret service dude in the car behind him or from the grassy knoll. Unless I can take pictures, who would believe me? Note to self: another theory to test. What would the ramifications to history be? I can't stop the assignation, and trying would really fuck things up. After making sure Abe lives, watching someone die doesn't sound very appealing.

2. Charles Lindbergh baby - Another case of watching a terrible crime. In the end, Bruno Hauptmann still has to die. Save the baby and all

hell breaks loose. Besides, Dmitri said to watch, not become a super hero and save people who die from unnatural causes. I have a mental image of Andy Kaufman singing the Mighty Mouse song "Here I Come to Save the Day."

3. Visit Tim and Kitt – I am not sure I could recover from seeing them. It scares me to think about it. I am afraid my mind and heart wouldn't want to come back to the present. I think it is better to leave the predictable heartache out of my travels, for now.

4. Music – I love me some blues from the 30's or more rock n' roll in the 60's. If I were in the same room as the Beatles, I would probably piss my pants with excitement. There's a thought,"Hey Paul, where did that puddle come from?" I will have to test this to see if I can leave anything behind. It's a good thing I didn't drop my flashlight beside Abe. That would have been as bad as leaving a Zippo lighter with the cave men.

5. Nixon – What else is there to learn? Why would I want to watch government corruption at its finest? This country hasn't had the same values since Tricky Dick. Watergate brought it to the forefront, just like an ugly pimple ready to pop. Does status quo make it right? I would love to change some things in history but how would that

change the world? Abe died a few months earlier than history told us, and it brought the civil rights movement into my life.

6. Jesus – Is that a question I really want to answer? Do I want to learn the truth? What if I observe something that changes everything I have ever been told about Jesus or religion? I don't want to alter, question or harm my private relationship with God. I hope I never take a trip that makes me feel that way. I can and I have been my own worst enemy at certain points in my life.

After a couple hours of research, I have decided to go on a people watching trip. There is something to be learned at *any* given time.

Lin's business deal will be here within the hour. It is time for me to get my ass off the couch and move.

Dinner in the oven? Check. Lin in wrench heaven? Check. Hot water calling my name? Check.

Just as I get out of the shower, I hear a big diesel truck pull up in the driveway. If there is one thing I know about my man, when he is around someone who enjoys bikes or cranes as much as he does, it will be an enjoyable two hour conversation.

Time for me to get comfy and visit the

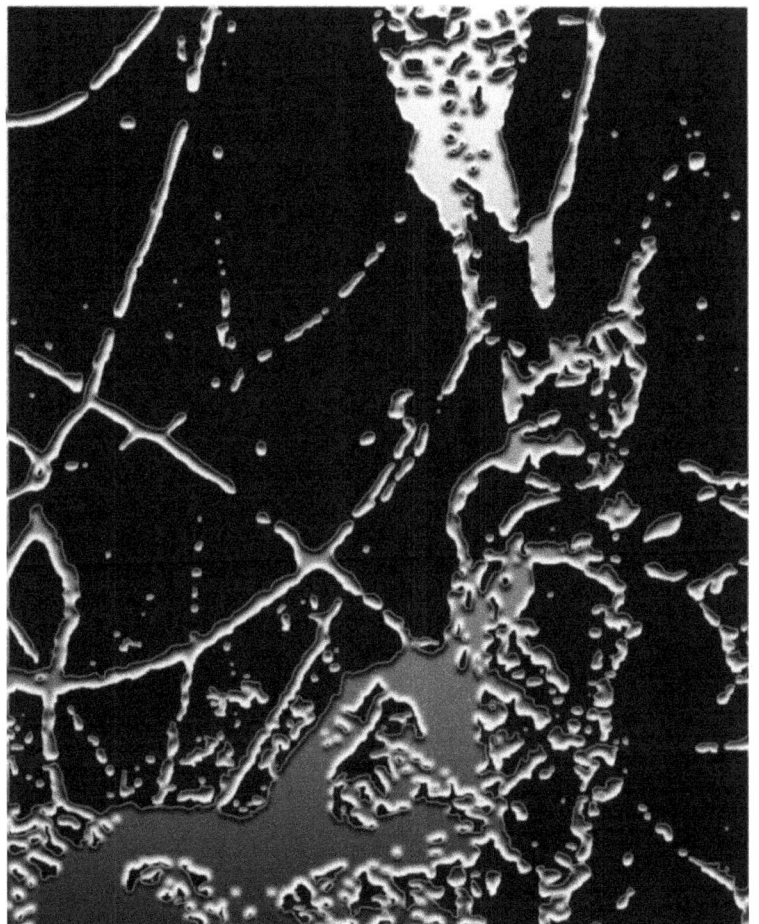

Chapter Sixteen

P eabody Hotel.

I'm going "Walkin in Memphis" circa 1935. I picked this place with a little help from the radio in the garage (shout out to Marc Cohen). I selected the year my Dad was born as a tribute to him. I have been to this city a couple of times. It is a great place to explore history, be it music, industry or people. Back in the day, before my kids, I had a great time camping at the state park here with Benedict, Ann, and Tim. Lying on the banks of the Mississippi, watching Fourth of July fireworks, is a memory I will never forget.

This is what I am talking about! I am on the roof of a very tall building, with a beautiful evening sky. I hear a big band "givin her hell" at one end of the roof. They've got that swing thing going on. I see an ocean of dancing young people. Man, they are having a good time! A big round dance floor surrounded by tables planted right in front of the band. I like big band music, but it is not on my top five list of "it's got a good beat and you can dance to it". As I get closer to the band the music starts to slow down, and I hear an incredible smooth female voice crooning out a "grab your baby and hold her tight" song. She sounds more like Sade then Billie Holiday.

I have fun walking around listening to the couples talk to each other, and all of the stupid pick up lines and snickering gossip.

"I heard she let him go to second base. Now look at her pressing up against Jeffery like Robert means nothing", one girl says.

There is Mr. Bo-Hunk, staggering around passing off his cheesy lines to all of the girls. The ladies seem to be less than amused and ignore him or tell him to get lost. You know the type, the package is pretty but open it up and all you find is someone wearing a stained wife-beater tee-shirt, living in the town junkyard in 20 years. He isn't so pretty anymore. The song will be over before this poor guy gets someone to dance with him. I don't think this dude could even dance if he wanted to. Damn, he can barely walk! Memphis does not equal big band music; I love me some Delta blues. I am outta here.

Damn how times have changed. The elevator doors open and out rolls this huge cloud of smoke. This is good for me, because no one steps forward to get in. Everyone actually takes a step back. Oh, wait a minute, these kids have never been in a 1973 Impala parked in a high school parking lot before school. Suckers! Sweet, no side-stepping to keep from bumping into people. You know the saying "the devil made me do it?" What can I say I can't help myself.

Mr. Cigar Puffer becomes my target for a little "fucking with." He seems to be very pleased with himself and works up the cigar cherry into a bright red glow. Just as he exhales this huge cloud of smoke, I step right in front of him and gently blow, giving him one major eye-hit. As he waves away the smoke and wipes his eyes, I pluck out his red carnation and drop it to the floor. Oh I'm not done yet, I can't resist flipping his hat onto the floor, lifting up his coat tail, and untucking his shirt when he bends over to pick up his personal belongings. When the doors finally open, Mr. Big n'Puffy is all kinds of flustered, trying to put himself back together before anyone notices. It almost gives me the feeling of watching an old black and white slap stick comedy only it's in color. I expect the Keystone Cops or Three Stooges to pop out any minute.

   Tuning in to what is going on around me, I hear a water fountain. I must have gotten here just in time for dinner because all of these people have their "going out" clothes on. The ladies are dressed to the nines and the men are all in tuxedos. I am not feeling a very good vibe. It all seems to be uptight and stuffy. I can almost see a nasty haze of bullshit floating through the air. Funny how that seems to suck up the clean oxygen that is left to breath. It's like everyone is out to impress the other guy be it with facts or fiction. The only thing that feels real are the ducks and turtles in the fountain. They are just minding their own business until it is time to go back into their cages.

The scenery is absolutely breathtaking. The lobby is at least two stories tall and no expense was spared. Everything appears to be very plush, polished, and shiny. It almost pushes one step short of gaudy, but still lingers in the "classy" realm.

I wonder around, listening to many conversations going on. There is a small group of five men. What is it with the cigars? All of them but one has a log sticking out of his mouth.

"The Germans now have their own Air Force called Luftwaffe. I would not be surprised to find out they had something to do with that plane hitting the Empire State building. Mark my words boys. This Hitler feller is going to be bad news for this here country." one says.

Now that is the understatement of the year, possibly the century!

I hear tidbits about Babe Ruth being "all washed up." How FDR is going to "hide all of the gold at a place called Fort Knox somewhere in Kentucky" and how a "darkie" named Jesse Owens is breaking track and field records.

Most of these people must be here for some sort of a convention, because when dinner is announced they all head to the dining room. Cattle call, anyone? Just as I am walking out the door I hear the fading voice of a young girl exclaim "Daddy says if we get a good cotton crop this year he will buy me a…"

It is time for me to let my feet walk on Beale Street. It is a beautiful warm evening as I head south on Third Street. It doesn't take long before I am entering a different world. When I get to Gayoso Street, I turn west, to reach the "red hot and low down" part of town. Talk about pick-up lines. I hear a female voice from the shadows,"Come on Sugar let Mama takes good care of you." Oh, the world's oldest profession. I venture to bet that no matter what place in time I decide to visit, I will always be able to find a whorehouse. Some things will never change, no matter how hard we try. Sex and money are way up on that list. The strange thing about that is, they can both kill you, or make you feel the best you have ever felt. Leaving you always wanting more of that instant gratification.

I love the old-time neon lights. There is something to be said for keeping it simple. LED lights lack the low hum of neon. It's like modern technology has taken the life out of lights. I don't see many uptight businessmen looking for a good time. I do, however, see a couple fancy suits trying to be discreet about what they are up to. There are many small groups of young people looking to blow off steam. I am noticing that the color is mixed. Were there any colored people at the Peabody? It hadn't occurred to me to even notice. I should have stepped back, and looked at the big picture. I paid too much attention to the small groups and the individual people.

The streets aren't so crowed that I can't walk at my usual fast pace. When I get to Second Street, I turn south; two or three more blocks and I will be on Beale. The closer I get, the darker it becomes. I mean that in more ways than one. I don't see anything that scares me. I see people lining up to get into a movie. They have the choice of "The Raven" starring Boris Karloff or "No More Ladies" with Mommie Dearest herself, Joan Crawford. The restaurants are serving dinner. The posted menus range from steak to catfish, and of course the specialty is Bar-B-Q. I walk past a couple of bars and pool halls with signs that state "colored only". I am surprised by all of the bright colors. There are advertisements hanging all over the place. I see Burma Shave, Wrigley's gum, and Redman chewing tobacco. There are also signs for when the next meal will be served at the local soup kitchen.

There are just as many people hanging out on the sidewalks as there are inside each business. There are guys just shooting the shit and enjoying each other's company. Some of them even brought chairs out onto the pavement. It is staggering, some of the conversations men have, when there are no women around. Don't misunderstand me; everything is not a bed of roses. I do see the ramifications of a depression still going on. I do see people begging and hungry. Everyone seems to be wearing their best, but their best is starting to show age. Most of them appear to want to "worry about that tomorrow". Tonight, they are going to have a good time.

I can hear me some blues getting closer with each step I take. Now, I am standing in front of Schwab's drug store. It's hard to believe! Fifty years from now, I will be standing in this very spot again with my feet facing west, looking at Beale Street. The store will look the same, but different. The advertisements in the window say it all. You can buy Noxzema for 49 cents, and it's in the big blue glass jar they used to have. Two rolls of toilet paper for 9 cents. Wow, while you may not understand skin care products, everybody gets shit paper. The view of Beale is also the same, but different. The lighting, and in general, the looks are different, but the shift in my soul is the same. In my day, it's all nice and put together for tourists. What I see before me now is meant for those who need the feeling that only the blues can give, the deep down moan of a soul coming out with each note.

Almost every corner has a musician either setting up or already get'n down with it. There is no sexual discrimination here. I stop to listen to a girl no bigger than a minute sing, and damn she is moaning loud and clear. I don't care what they say, you can't sing like that unless God has dealt you some shit. I listen to her sing a couple of songs, and while trying to decide what to play next, a man steps out of the small crowd and whispers in her ear. Mr. Man is not requesting a song. He has a little something else on his mind. Mr. Man must want a quickie, because she leaves a couple of guys playing on without her. They just give her a nod and a wink while their fingers keep on picking. I wonder if they get a cut of the proceeds. Bless her heart. That is sad. Now I know where her sound comes from.

A couple corners down I hear a smooth, high-pitched male voice. I weave my way through the people standing around listening to him belt it out. I see a man leaning over his guitar. All I can see are his long-fingered black hands picking and bending the strings. The sound coming from him is pure, uncut, sorrowful blues. The people listening are caught up in the trance, swaying back and forth with an occasional "Amen", "tell it" or "ah-ha" thrown in. Oh hell no! I have heard this song before! It starts with a high note pick and the "I'm gonna git up in the mornin', I believe I dust my broom…" It can't be who I think it is? Oh shit, is this Robert Johnson? Come on dude, lift your head. He is so into the raw sound he is making, I don't get to see his face until the song is over. Before me is the beautiful black face with a brilliant smile. Ok, the left eye is a little droopy, just like the two known pictures of him. All my hopes are dashed when I hear him tell someone his name is Robert Spencer. This guy must be a good copycat, and has obviously seen Mr. Johnson. He has it dialed in right down to his sound and his song. I'm moving on, not much for seeing "wanna-bes". If I can't have the real thing, piss on it. Next.

Towards the intersection of Front Street I have the pleasure of hearing an upbeat jug band. There is even a little boy getting down with some really good dance moves. It has a southern feel, and makes me want to tap my toes. This little guy has got it going on and he loves the attention. His dad must be the one blowing into the big ceramic jug, because when the song is done the boy runs over and gives him a big hug. Then, he darts off to pick up the few coins tossed onto the ground for him. The wind blows out of his sails when he sees his mom has come to pick him up. Parked behind her is an old, beat-up pickup truck. Three kids are in the back. They look to be between eight and 11. In the front seat is an older woman and a young boy. The boy looks like he is about 14, and he is the one driving. Our little footloose friend doesn't want to go home, but he does as he is told. Mom puts her hands on her hips and gives him the look. That is all it takes. The older woman opens the truck door, and he jumps in without a fuss. I am going to see where they go. I pop my ass on the tailgate, beside mom, and away we go.

We travel the same direction from which I just came. As we pass, I see "Miss Thing" is back to singing. Mr. Man was short, sweet and straight to the point! "If you have an erection lasting longer than 4 hours…"

The kids in the back of the truck don't say 10 words. They all look like they are tired and ready for bed. What have these kids been doing all day to make them this tired? We go on for what feels like miles. We are definitely not in the city anymore. We pass tiny little share cropper houses with an occasional person sitting on a front porch. The little lonely shacks are few and far between. If there is a light on, it radiates from one kerosene lamp. Most of the houses are dark and tucked in for the night. We stop at a house that looks no different from the rest. We all pile out of the truck and the mother instructs her kids to, "Wash up and get to bed. No workin tomorrow. We got church."

We go inside the house, it consists of three rooms. A kitchen with a blanket hanging up makes rooms one and two. Off of the kitchen is a bedroom. The bathroom must be outside. The kids do as they are told, and wash their hands and face in a water basin sitting on a big table. The kitchen is full, but clean. I love the old milk bottle complete with daisies in the middle of the table. Against one wall is a very small counter and three overhead cabinets. The wall opposite the blanket wall has a cast iron wood burning stove. The last wall has a small table that is covered with tin storage containers, a basket of green peppers, and miscellaneous kitchen items. There are a few iron skillets and pans hanging on the wall. The room is a little warm, but not so stifling that I can't breathe. I can tell the stove has not been burning for a while. The three kids, and the driver, follow the older woman, who must be Grandma, into the room behind the blanket. I see two small, full-sized beds that take up all of the space. The beds are lined up end to end. The little girl crawls in bed with Granny and the three boys pile into the other bed. Our little dancing buddy must sleep in the other room with Mom and Dad. Their bedroom is same size as the whole kitchen blanket room. It contains a full bed, a twin sized bed, and a bureau of drawers. There is a small closet that must hold the entire family's' wardrobe. Despite the size, I am impressed with how clean everything is. These two ladies may not have much, but what they do have they are proud of, and it shows. I decide to beat feet when Momma picks up the kerosene lamp with one hand and the dancing youngster with the other to call it a day.

I better do the same. I have been gone for awhile now. I will have to get more comfortable with my time and the risk of getting caught. The longest trip I have taken so far has been to Monterey. The time is coming when I will have days to explore. The sooner I take care of business, the sooner I can make this happen. Step one has already been taken when I told the guys I

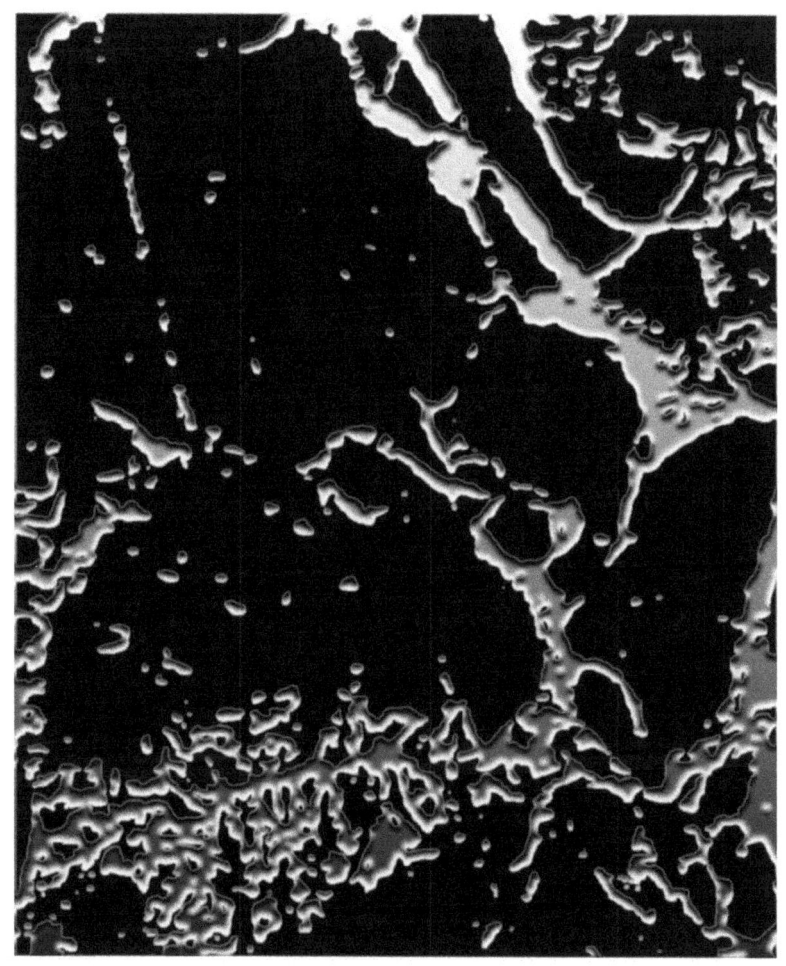

Chapter Seventeen

Quit my job.

There is a thought that isn't fun to come back to. The interviewing process begins tomorrow and I am not looking forward to it. Michael and Eric have been great since I told them about our plan. I am eager to start the new adventure on my terms, but this is what I have done for the better part of my life. I am a born bean counter. Damn that black and white world!

Lin and "Dude Man" are getting to the end of wheeling and dealing on the bike. It sounds like we may have just sold a motorcycle. Camper shopping here we come! Just when I think he is about to leave, with the bike all loaded up, Lin starts talking about an old part he found at a swap meet. They both head for the garage, on a mission. Oh shit, there they go for another hour. I go inside and turn the oven to warm so dinner doesn't consist of burnt baked chicken stuffed with charred rice.

While waiting for Lin, I decide to do a little research on Robert Johnson. I can't shake the feeling that I actually saw him play and heard his moan on this last trip. I discover that yes, he was in Memphis in 1935 and yes, he did change his name every once in awhile. Looking at the picture taken at the Hooks photography place around that same time, I would bet my life that the man I saw was Robert Johnson. It is remarkable how few documented facts there are about him. Talk about getting lost in your own story, what is real and what isn't? All of the legends and stories he had to live up to in 27 short years of life. Is it a tragedy or a triumph to be more notable after you die then when you were alive?

Six months have gone by in a snap. Lin is gone and working in Houston, Henry is done with his senior year, and Allen is going to become a Daddy any day now. Thomas and Poppy are enjoying their young life with three cats. Nichole has a new boyfriend that I can't figure out. To her he is Mr. Dream Man and can do no wrong, but Lin and I aren't so sure. We hope we are wrong or that Nichole will open her eyes before it is too late. She is a smart girl but right now she is not listening to anyone. Let's see how many jobs he has to quit (while she works two jobs) before she realizes something isn't right here. He seems nice enough, but infinitely lazy.

I have one more week at the office. My replacement Maryanne, seems to have moved right in and I have every confidence she will do a great job. Bless her heart, she is slowly learning that you have to speak up if you want to be heard. Sitting back waiting for something to happen isn't going to get her very far. If she goes in with facts, the rest of the shit will fall into place.

Every room in the house has a fresh coat of paint and most of the personal items have been boxed up to be sent to storage. The most time-consuming work was refinishing the floors. It has been a lot of work, but damn the floors look great, even if I do say so myself! Our next house had better have wood floors or I will get to do it again. I don't care much for carpets, they are just expensive cootie collectors. I had to bust ass to have this house done for Henry's graduation party. I killed two birds with one stone and now the house is ready to sell. I have not sold a house in over 20 years. This is the only home Henry has ever known. That is why I waited until he was ready to leave the nest before I even attempted to sell it. It's a good thing we have an awesome real estate agent that knows what she is doing.

I have mastered the art of taking small trips while I am in the shower. I have figured out that if I sit down in the shower I can have a few minutes without interruption. It has really been a Godsend to escape for a few minutes. This "get shit done" on steroids lifestyle has been draining, both physically and mentally.

I watched Martin Luther King give his "I have a dream" speech. I stood in the middle of the reflecting pool so I wouldn't have to piss with people. It was everything I imagined it would be. The collective silence to hear one man speak gave me goose bumps. The statue of Abraham Lincoln behind him made it that much more powerful. I think Mr. King had a beautiful vision. I wonder what would have happened to the civil rights movement if he had not been assassinated. Could he have done more as a man than he did as a martyr? It was breathtaking to see this historical event in color. I hope I never get tired of that. I love the depth and realness color brings. When you watch things in black and white do you ever assume that is how the world of that time looked?

I visited a few concerts. I saw the Beatles at Shea Stadium, Led Zeppelin, Stevie Ray Vaughan, and Godsmack with Staind.

Led Zepplin was fucking great! Talk about getting a contact buzz! Man, all I had to do to get stoned was inhale deep and hold it. John Bonham was a monster on the drums. Why is it all great drummers do it with their mouths too? Take notice next time you see an amazing drummer his mouth will be moving to keep rhythm. Being invisible gave me the opportunity to stand right in front of Bonham's drum kit as he beat the hell out of it. Now I know why many lead singers like to face the drums. The vibrations were moving, literally moving my guts whether I wanted them to or not. John Paul Jones appeared to be either really stoned, or bored out of his mind. Feeling the vibe come off of Robert Plant was pure sex. It made sense why the band called him "Percy". He strutted around like a male peacock. Mr. Jimmy Page was in a world all of his own when he played, and always moving. Fuck the radio version of "Stairway to Heaven". I got to hear it live…OMG! I don't know where we were but the venue was huge and there were thousands of people. I bet less than half of them remembered the concert the next day.

   The Beatles at Shea was awful. I didn't stick around long. It was one constant, massive, high-pitched scream. They weren't in tune with each other and it showed. You can't blame them with all of that noise. They could have come out and sang Mary Had a Little Lamb. No one would have cared or even heard it. No wonder they quit doing live concerts. Why fucking bother if you can't hear the music? One day, I will visit John at his home, or maybe go to Abby Road, and watch the magic happen first-hand.

   The Stevie Ray trip wasn't really a concert but a sound check session. No theatrics there folks! What you hear is what you get. This man was lost to many young ears and eyes that never got to see the phenomenon of Stevie live. Just to watch his fingers bend a string and see him close his eyes when he sinks into his sound was orgasmic. I stood right in front of him trying to absorb some of this way-down-soul-moving vibe. I could smell his tooth paste, mixed with cigarettes. I determined the best way to feel Stevie was to take a step back and watch him fade into his own rhythm. It was almost like the guitar sucked him in and the rest of the world vanished. When he wasn't playing he seemed to be a really down-to-earth guy, leaning almost towards shy. None of that "please worship me because I am great" bullshit. He was just a simple man loving his sound in blue jeans and cowboy boots. Okay, maybe a little flashy, with the hat and fur overcoat. He was definitely one of those people that when he laughed, it came straight from his toes. I couldn't help but laugh with him.

The Godsmack and Staind show was one I had to revisit because I loved it so much the first time. Love me some Sully and Aaron! Once again, I don't know where we were but it wasn't the Coliseum. I guess that was a good thing, I wonder if I can run into myself on these trips? That can't be good, no matter how I slice it. It was amazing to feel the energy between Sully and Shannon when they had the drum battle. Unlike the first time, my ass was right on stage. I love the smell of a clean sweaty man. Most of the time, it is intoxicating. There is a huge difference between a good natural man smell, and just stinking. The competition between them was fierce. Even if they have done it a thousand times, I could still feel it.

A couple other trips I made didn't involve music but rather sports. I went back to watch Michael Jordan and Walter Payton play their games. Nobody, I mean nobody (ya hear me, Labron?) can do what Michael did on the court. Talk about loving me some man smell! Damn, baby, he smells like raw energy. What I never noticed on television was Michael's mouth going all the time. He talked shit, but it is more like getting into his components head saying "You want it? You better bring it or go home" shit. I don't want to know what he is like off of the court. I would rather keep the image I have and watch him create poetry with a basketball. It was fun to watch that whole team play together again. Hit that three pointer, Mr. Steve Kerr, and watch Dennis punish anyone who tried to keep him from getting a board. The man may be a freak (let your freak flag fly, dude) but he got real fucking ugly when it came to rebounds.

I feel the same way about Walter. I don't want to know what kind of man he was outside of a Bears uniform. Show me a man that can take the abuse on the field that he took and still pop up from the bottom of the pile. I got on the field during the game. I couldn't do that with basketball, too much bobbing and weaving, or plain old "get the fuck out of the way" happening there. At least with football, most of the guys were going in one direction. A couple of interceptions made me pay attention and move quick. I am here to tell you, Richard Dent is one big man! Talk about getting a team motivated! All anyone would have to do is look into Mike Singletary's wild, intense eyes.

The huddle was a really cool experience. "Ya gonna get that mother fucker off my back or just stand there holding your dick?" "Hey Jimmy ya think you can get the ball to me or are you gonna hold it all day?" Back in the day, watching these games on TV, I never realized how many times McMahon called audibles. Ditka would get pissed on the sidelines but nine times out of 10 Jimmy was right.

The whole 1985 Chicago Bears team was a force to be reckoned with. So much talent and just shear fucking hunger. I bet a poll would show that more women than men watched football in 1985, because the team took the fan with them on the journey. Remember the "Superbowl Shuffle" and McMahon with his "in your face, kiss my ass" attitude? He was either fighting with Rozelle or mooning a helicopter!

I plan on going back for a few more games. I really miss the energy of watching magic happen. I quit watching the NBA when Michael retired, and the NFL when Walter Payton retired. Now I have the opportunity to see them live, and go where ever I want. I can have "smell-a vision". What can I tell ya? I love smells! I haven't done the locker room thing yet, but it isn't high on my list of short trips. Seeing my heroes naked just isn't right. It is almost like seeing Superman take a shit. No thanks!

I have finally reached a slow point, hence I have the time to write this shit down. I scribble little notes after every trip and have gotten better about writing while on my journey. Sometimes I get so caught up in it that I forget to document. I have no plans for the upcoming weekend and Henry is going to be gone until Sunday evening. I think I need to make a long trip and see if I can break my record. Where do I want to spend hours sucking up the past?

Henry left about an hour ago and I have talked to Lin. I told him I was going to be spending a quiet day with a book and my cell phone will be off.

I am sitting on our bed with the door locked. I have everything I need in my trusty bag. I packed some extra tissues because this trip may tug at my heart strings. Against the advice Dmitri gave me, I am ready to go on a long journey into the realm of

Chapter Eighteen

R_{eal.}

I instantly recognize where I am. There is the two-room cabin and over there is the bunk house. What a cool little building, just four bunks and a wood burning stove on the inside. I am in West Virginia and this is my grandparents' hunting cabin. What a beautiful place on the top of a mountain. To get to the top, you have to drive up a long muddy dirt road. There are no guard rails so patience is an absolute if someone is coming from the opposite direction. This is literally a one-lane path. I don't remember ever hearing anyone bitch about the driveway. How could you? Open your eyes here and you will believe in God.

I can see cows off in the distance; they are minding their own business, munching on grass. They seem very content among the many trees. I see the long swinging cattle gate that keeps them in. One has to jump out of the car to open it so they can drive through, then close it right away so the cows don't get out. There is plenty of room to share with the cows. They usually stay away from the cabin, but heaven help if you step in one of the "pies" they leave behind.

Over there is the outhouse. In the winter if you flip a switch on the porch a heater would turn on inside the outhouse so you didn't freeze your ass off while you answer natures' call. I absolutely hated going to the bathroom in there when I was a kid. I always felt like a snake was going to jump up and bite me on the ass. I perfected the art of "hovering" while peeing. Coming here as a child was always a treat, playing in the river, catching crawdads and mud puppies all day. Eating Grandma's incredible cooking in the evening; damn that woman could cook anything. Ending the day listening to the night critters outside, and Grandpa snoring, as I went to sleep snuggled up to my sister in a tiny little twin bed was wonderful.

Now the sun is just starting to come up, and the birds are singing. The dew is still wet on the ground and in the air. I suck in a big breath full, it doesn't get any better than this. Fuck the pumped-in oxygen in Vegas. Give me this every day, cows and all! I can hear the river running over the rocks. It could be 110 degrees outside, but that water is always ice cold because it comes straight off of the mountain. I can smell sausage cooking. Sure enough, I see Grandma Vivian in the kitchen window making breakfast. What a wonderful woman. She always made her opinion known in her own quiet way. Tough n' Classy is how I describe her. Grandpa Orville just walked outside with a bucket of food for his hunting dogs. Look at him go! I haven't seen him move that fast in years; taking care of business and getting it done. I would describe him as a gruff John Wayne-type. When he told you to do something, you did it. Let's just say it was wise to be well-behaved around Grandpa at all times. When Kitt got sick, I saw a softer side to Orville. Both of my grandparents were right there by her bedside for months, with much love and a strong devotion to make her comfortable. After Kitt died, I had a special relationship with my Grandpa. Orville went to two weddings in his lifetime, his and mine. That is saying something, considering I have six aunt and uncles.

Wow, there is Big Red! That damn dog used to slobber all over my legs when we had to take him for a walk. Kitt and I used to argue about who had to hold that leash, neither one of us wanted to walk him. I usually won, one of the perks of being "Big Sis". If we wanted to go swimming with our brother, Dean, we would have to walk the dogs for an hour first. There were at least four dogs. Grandpa liked Redbones, Walkers and Blue Tics. I don't remember any of the others' names, just Red. Fucking slobber. YUCK!

Oh my God, my heart has just stopped beating. Kitt comes running out of the cabin, chasing after Grandpa because she wants to "help". Look at those little legs move! Of course, no shoes. My sweet, sweet sister. An uncontrollable wave of emotion comes over me and I start to cry from my soul. I am on my knees, gasping for breath. My heart feels like it is three times bigger than it should be. My chest physically hurts. I miss seeing that sweet face! Get a grip! Deep breaths, Molly, suck and hold. Again, suck and hold. In through the nose. Out through the mouth, Molly. Come on, you've got this.

After I wipe my face, I can see. I notice Kitt is holding Grandpa's hand while they watch the dogs eat breakfast. She looks to be about five-ish. She is sporting the short, pixie haircut Mom gave us both. I basically refused to comb my hair so mom cut it all off. Who had time to worry about hair? There were better things to do, like playing outside. We weren't allowed to love on the dogs because their purpose was to hunt. I used to love to hear them sing. I never went hunting with Grandpa. The thought of killing an animal is completely repulsive to me. Shit, I carry bugs and spiders outside instead of stepping on them. If you are going to hunt, that is fine, as long as you eat what you kill. If you hurt just for the sheer sport of killing something, then you need to be taken out back and beat! If you eat your kill, than it is all part of the circle of life. The thought of eating a spider just because I can kill it doesn't make any sense. It's not part of my food chain. Period.

Kitt and Grandpa walk up by the river and she is telling him about the swimming hole she and "Big Sissy" are going to build there today. Wait a minute, I am here? As much as I want to stand here and look into that sweet little face, I have to see if I can see myself. There is just one vehicle in the driveway. That means Mom and Dad aren't here. It is too early in the morning to be running an errand.

Kitt breaks away and starts running back to the cabin. Grandma tells her to "Wash your hands after being out there with those nasty dogs". I watch as Kitt pushes a step stool over to the sink and does as she is told. The running water is just a trickle because the incoming water supply is from a black pipe placed in the river. No modern conveniences here folks, but as a kid this place was great! Nothing but vast spaces of pure nature to play in until your heart is content. Just watch out for snakes.

There is a memory I can still see in my minds eye. This memory is 45 years old at this point. Kitt had left her shoes on the other side of the cattle gate. Me being "Big Sissy", I went to get them for her. Of course I never (and still don't) wear shoes, unless it is because of the weather or someone has a stupid rule. What can I tell ya? My toes can't breathe! Anyway, just as I put my foot down, all I can remember is a huge white mouth with long sharp looking fangs. The next thing I recall is Mom smacking my cheeks and Grandma checking my feet to confirm I had not been bitten. I don't know to this day if I climbed the gate, jumped over it or crawled through it. If I close my eyes I can see it as if I were looking at a photograph. They say pot is bad for the memory, but I think not. I say having a lazy mind is bad for the memory.

The kitchen used to be a porch before my uncles closed it in for Grandma. Suddenly, I hear Grandma say

"Molly, it is time for you to get up and get your bed made." Kitt disappears into the one and only other room. There are no closets in this room, just three beds (two full and a twin) and a beat up couch with a couple of chairs. There are hooks on the walls to hang things up. There are a couple of gun racks, since this is a hunting cabin. I never did understand the fascination of hanging a deer head on the wall. Nothing real fancy here, but it feels cozy and warm. I can hear Kitt saying "Come on Big Sissy, let's play outside. Grandma says you have to get up now. Come on, she made breakfast."

Grandpa comes walking back into the house and he is ready to eat. He barks out "Molly, get your feet on the floor and let's eat." Some things never change. If you play hard you also sleep hard. I can hear myself grunting as I pull myself out of bed. I hear Kitt and I hear me start to giggle. It sounds like she is helping me make the bed and something happened to make us laugh. It's almost like hearing a tape recording of your own voice. I don't have this memory, so I don't know what we are up to. I notice the sound of two girls being silly even makes Orville laugh, Grandma is just shaking her head with a big smile on her face.

Kitt comes back into the kitchen when she hears Grandpa's voice bark out, "Come on girls, it's getting cold". Damn that girl could eat. When we were little, Kitt would clean off your plate if you didn't want it. It takes everything she has to pull the chair out from the table so she can sit down. The effort even makes her tongue stick out. We were not allowed to put our elbows on the table. We also didn't speak unless we were asked a question. Children were to be seen, not heard, at the table. Orville is losing his patience and Grandma is taking off her apron. I hear my feet hit the floor and head in my direction. This is the moment! What do I look like? Come on, Molly, let me

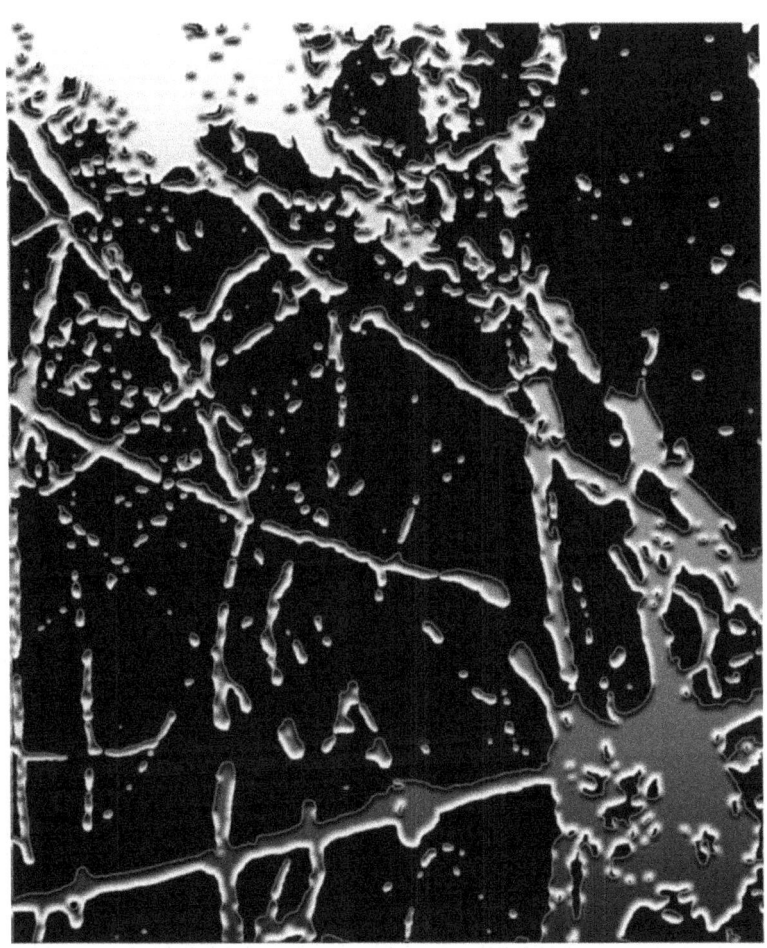

Chapter Nineteen

S ee Me.

Wait a fucking minute! I am sitting in my bedroom. I am back to point "A". The charm is dangling from my bracelet, sparkling at me. I feel like it is laughing at me, little fucker!

Just as I am about to see myself. BOOM! I am here. Can I see myself? Is there some physics thing working here? Things that make you go hmmmm. There is only one way to find out. Time for a test.

Time to take a

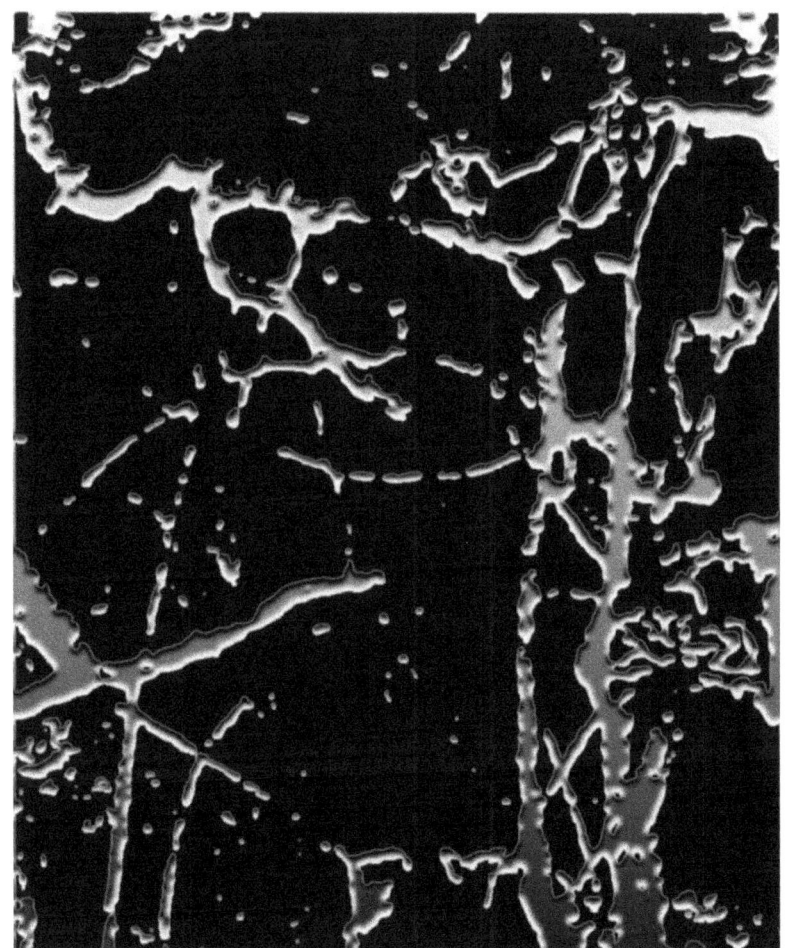

Chapter Twenty

T rip down home.

Wow, I have so many good memories here. What is it with me and early mornings? Again, the sun is coming up, and I am digging the fresh air. Everything is so green and pretty with flowers in full bloom. I am standing on the cement "hump" bridge that covers the creek. This bridge washed out in the 70's and was replaced with a railroad tie bridge. Granny's house is right in front of me. I can remember when Fat Ma and Pawpaw Wash, my great grandparents had a little store in this house. That was when Granny lived up on the hill, and before Russell was born. This tells me the time frame I have landed in. There is a light on in the kitchen.

There is the water well. A stone box is built around the opening and a big metal lid covers it. The water that comes out of that well is the nectar of the Gods. As kids, we loved it when Granny needed water because it meant we got to fill up the bucket. Grandpa was always right there to make sure we didn't fall in. The porch has an old ringer washer in the corner. I can hear her now "You young'uns get away before you get your arm caught!"

There is Grandpa's chair, an old green wooden frame with woven leather straps that make the seat. I have always loved this porch. The family usually gathered here in the evenings to shoot the shit or play a card game called Rook. I could never figure out how that damn game was played. If we were lucky, there would be some Stanley Brothers music playing. I do not like country music, but bluegrass at Granny's goes together like peanut butter and jelly. Throw in a little Lester and Earl, now we have a party.

While I am deep in memoryland, the front door opens and out walks my Granny with steam coming off her cup of coffee. What a naturally beautiful woman. She is up and dressed, ready for the day, while everyone else is still asleep. Kitt and I used to beg her to let her gorgeous long black hair down so we could brush it. She always wore it in a bun but when it was down she could sit on it. I can smell breakfast and I see she is wearing her apron. I hear a deep voice following Granny when she turns back towards the house and says, "Ya'all can go squirrel huntin' tomorrow. Today, we have everybody comin' in." Suddenly, I see my Dad standing in the doorway. He responds "You just tell me what you need Mommy and we'll get it done."

What a big man my Dad was; is. No wonder all of my boyfriends were afraid of him. He has the same beautiful coloring and black hair that Granny has. He looks so young and handsome. Dad loved being down home with his family. When we would drive down the closer we got to home, the more he would whistle bluegrass tunes. Give him a half an hour and he would get his southern drawl back. I think my Dad was always a "momma's boy"; he adored his mother and loved to get up to spend quiet time with her. Granny taught him to cook and I am here to tell you he was a wonderful cook. We ate great Hillbilly food growing up. There is nothing better than a pot of soup beans (that's brown beans, not the Yankee white ones) and pone of cornbread with fried cabbage or potatoes on the side. Dad always had a huge garden and we ate vegetables like they were going out of style. You name it, he grew it. Some of my best lunches consisted of a trip to the garden with a water hose, paper towel, salt shaker, and a knife.

I wish he could give me one of his bear hugs right now. I think I would probably just melt right here. Dad and Grandma take a seat to enjoy their coffee in the stunning silence for a minute. I can tell by the look on my Dad's face that he is 100% content right now. He starts to whistle an old Hank Williams tune called "I'm so lonesome I could cry." Wow, I miss hearing that. I start to cry and smile at the same time. Unexpectedly, I hear the words of the song being sung in a deep baritone voice, then out walks my Uncle Woodrow. We always called him Uncle Chuck. Granny is in hog heaven, a huge smile breaks out on her face. Two of her babies who moved away from the hills of Kentucky are now here, and giving her a concert. There are three things I could always count on at Granny's: lots of love, lots of food, and lots of music-unless the Wildcats were playing.

If there was a ballgame on, there was lots of yelling at the television. Heaven help you if you had a cross word to say about Joe B.

My Mom walks through the doorway, carrying my brother Russell. What a little fat, round butterball! My Mom looks so pretty, vibrant and young. Wow, is her hair piled up! I used to be able to find her in stores if I could see over the shelves. It isn't Marge Simpson high but, she kept Aqua Net in business. I can tell by the way she looks at my Dad that they are still in love and happy. I almost forgot what that looked like. They were divorced when I was 19 and it didn't end well, and that's all you need to know about it. If you want smut, you are reading the wrong story. Next.

Mom waits until the show is over and says to dad "Bob, if you take him, I'll help your Mom in the kitchen." She puts Russell down on the porch and off he goes towards Dad. Look at those little chubby, curved legs. Dad hasn't yet put him on a diet or in his special shoes that straighten out his bowed legs. I notice my Dad's chest. He is wearing a button up shirt, open, and he isn't wearing a t-shirt. This may seem to be an odd thing to notice, but he has all of his chest hair. My Dad was burned when I was small and some of his chest hair didn't grow back. Thanks to a man named Bob Durham, dad survived the accident with that as his only physical scar.

Granny gets up and wipes her hands with her apron as if to say "time to get busy." Mom and Granny lead the way back into the house. The men stay on the porch to bullshit with each other. I follow the ladies. It is just as I remember it, small, simple and clean. The television is on the right as I walk into the living room. It is one of those huge cabinets with a little television screen, by todays standards. On the same wall, on the other side of the kitchen doorway, is an old cabinet record player and shelves. Wow, there is the Jesus picture right where I remember it, and the little porcelain clock shaped like a Victorian carriage. A couch and chair are both facing the television. On the opposite wall is an open doorway leading to the bedrooms. I make an immediate right and am in the world's best smelling kitchen. There is the black pot-bellied stove, warm but not hot. Granny's wash basin of flour is on the table, which means she is making biscuits. Both of my Grandmothers had the biscuit-making down to a "melt in your mouth" science. I am not leaving here without eating at least one of those delightful morsels! I hear Mom tell Granny that she is going to go "get the girls," and she heads towards the back bedrooms.

If this trip plays out like the last one, I am about to "pop" forward. I am not ready to leave just yet. I want to see my Dad again. This may sound strange, but I want to smell his Old Spice. Have you ever thought about the things in life that make you feel safe? My Dad had two of these qualities, his smell and snoring at night. I always knew I was safe. Whatever made me wake up was just a bad dream and it was safe to go back to sleep.

As I walk back out on the porch, I notice the music has stopped and there is a deep conversation going on. I hear my Dad say, "Mommy wants me to take her to town later. I think I might try to see my kids." Uncle Chuck is silent for a second, then says, "What will Fran say if she finds out?" Dad gets a little grin and says, "I have a right to see my kids. She isn't going to find out, if you go with us and tell her you have a buddy you want to visit in Hindman. She won't think anything if we're gone for a couple hours."

My Uncle agrees to run block and help his brother out. Dad appears pleased with himself, and his plan. His face breaks out in a huge mischievous grin, right before the beautiful whistling falls back into place. Dad was always honest with me, but with my Mom, not so much. As life played out, neither of them were very honest with each other. Does this make them bad people? No it does not, only human with their unique flaws. Bottom line: I learned from my parents what I want to be. In the same respect, I learned in sometimes harsh ways, what I don't want to be or do. This is life, from the first generation to the last.

This is something I never knew. I am not going to go into a whole bunch of drama here, but in a nutshell, my Dad loved his other three children. I never knew he had to go to such extremes to get to see them. I didn't get to meet them until Granny passed away in 1984. I understand my Mom's jealousy. Any woman would be jealous given how my parents hooked up while being married to other people. Thank God they did, or I wouldn't exist. The blood and gore to that story is not for your reading pleasure, sorry. My Dad very much loved two women at the same time and it was something that haunted him until the day he died. Period. It feels kind of odd to see this side of my Dad. On one hand, it is very sad that he has to carry this private burden. He has to tell lies just so he can spend time with his kids. On the other hand it is like playing with fire should Mom find out. I loved my Mom very much but not when she was pissed off. The woman had a lot of Orville running through her veins.

   I walk across the porch and stand beside my Dad. Oh my God, I love that smell! I suck it in as hard as I can. Talk about feeling like I was 5 again. I am startled out of my smelling trance by my Mom coming back out on the porch. This time she is carrying Kitt, who has a major case of bed head and is rubbing her eyes to wake up. Mom tells Dad, "Here take her. I'll go get Molly up and dressed". Dad hands Russell over to my Uncle Chuck and takes Kitt on his lap. She proceeds to curl up and get comfy. I can't believe how cute she is. Damn, I miss that face!! If you didn't know my sister, then it is hard to explain her ever-good, sweet, natural beauty. She always had that quality even when she was pissed. I can count on one hand how many times I saw her angry enough to spit nails. It just wasn't in her nature.

   This trip has been a very nice walk down memory lane. I need to get back to business and solve the question I came here to solve. I have to go back into the house (through the kitchen to check on those biscuits) and see if I can see myself.

Granny is busy cooking. The table is covered with plates and bowls waiting to be filled with some of the best food. The house is starting to come to life. My aunts Jane and Ann, are helping Granny put everything on the table. Uncle Nelson has been to the same hair stylist Kitt went to. He staggers towards the coffee pot. Fat Ma and Pawpaw Wash are here now. It takes my breath away to see their faces again. I was really small when they passed and I only remember their faces from pictures. Fat Ma always had bubble gum in her apron pocket, and Pawpaw Wash had nickels in his pockets. That is a memory that makes me smile.

I see Mom walk out to the porch to get her other two chicks, but I am not with her. I must have gone out the side door because I hear me yelling "Come on Dad! Granny made biscuits." I hear Dad's deep laugh, the one he had when he was really tickled about something. I hear footsteps heading my way and make a mad dash for the hot pan of bread coming out of the oven. I scoop up one of Granny's dish towels, because this little piece of heaven is going to be hotter than hell. Just as I hear my running footsteps come into the living room, I reach for a biscuit. I look down at my hot little jewel and start to fold it

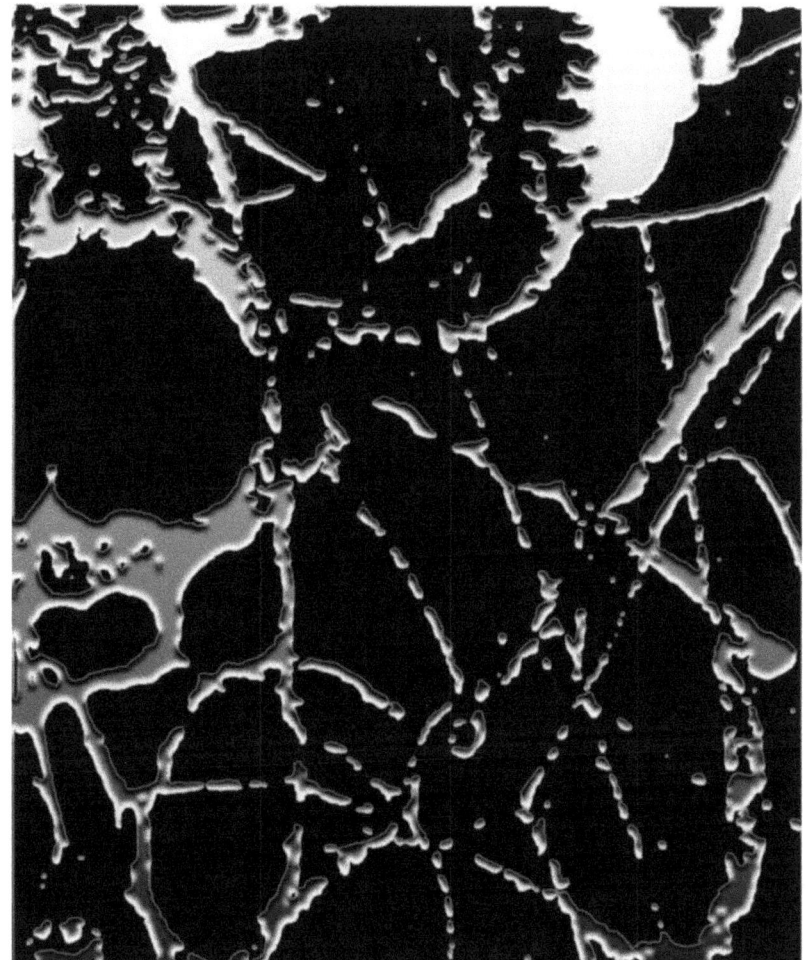

Chapter Twenty-one

U_{p in the towel.}

Damn it all straight to hell! I am back in my bedroom. I look down and there is no biscuit. What the hell? My mouth is still watering! It wasn't touching my skin. The towel is still warm and smells delicious. What the fuck! Over!

Ok, now I know, I cannot be in the same room with myself. I can live with that but I can't live with leaving that biscuit behind. I put the charm between my fingers and imagine Granny taking the bread out of the oven. I get nothing. I am still sitting on my bed, holding a warm dish towel. So, there is the brick wall to my travels. So much for reliving the best moments of my life.

I also know that my ass is tired. I haven't been gone very long, but the emotions involved seem to have left me dragging ass. What a double edge sword I have opened. I love seeing my family, hearing them talk, seeing them smile. But now my heart just wants more, more, more ("with a rebel yell"). I didn't care much for being there to see my Dad keep secrets from my Mom. As a parent, I understand why he did it. But as a wife, I would hate it if Lin did something like that. It is a good thing I respect and appreciate his only ex-wives that matter - the mothers of his children.

Going to Kentucky showed me something else, too. In West Virginia, I got to see Grandma, Grandpa and Kitt. All three have since passed away. At Granny Gibson's, Russell was the first family member I have seen that is still living today. My aunts and Uncle Nelson also still live in the beautiful hills. I never thought about this on the first trip. It seems the only limitation is that I cannot see myself. I will definitely go back to Kentucky. I would like to know my Uncle Sterling. I have always been told about his beautiful soul, his extremely high intelligence (he skipped ahead grades in school) and his make-your-sides-hurt sense of humor. He passed away right before Kitt was born. Granny had evidence that proved Sterling died from exposure to Agent Orange in Vietnam.

Right now, I am going to lay back and take a little cat nap. Just as I creep from twilight to sleep, the house phone rings. What the hell? Nobody calls the landline any more. The whole world revolves around cell phones. The only reason it is still hooked up is that it is more expensive to get the internet if I don't have a landline. It is Allen on the other end

"What the hell Mom, did you turn your cell phone off? You better get here because you are about to become a Grandma."

That's all it takes. I barely say goodbye to Allen and out the door I go. I cannot enter the hospital barefoot so back into the house I go…fucking rules!

Nicki is well into labor when I finally reach the hospital. I respectfully comply with her wishes and stay out of the delivery room. I know Nicki isn't comfortable with the whole world seeing her "junk", as she puts it. That is fine with me. I plant myself in the waiting room. Ok, "plant" may not be the right choice. I pace a little, sit a little, pace a lot, sit a little, sneak outside for a smoke, and pace in the parking lot. Allen is just beside himself with excitement. Talk about not being able to sit still! It makes me smile to myself, watching him. It reminds me of basketball coach Andy, warning Allen that if he ever drank a Mountain Dew before a ball game again, he was "personally going to kick his ass." Coach Andy, as a teenager, had been around Allen every day from the time he was eight weeks old. His mom used to babysit for Allen while I worked, so I know he said it with stern love.

Finally, Allen comes through the double doors with tears of joy running down his face. He walks over, without saying a word, and takes me by the hand to go see his beautiful son, Lennon. I never thought in a million years that I could instantly love someone as much as I love my children. My first look into that new, sweet little face is deep love at first sight. Lennon is more beautiful than any words can describe. I don't stay in the room long because the doctors are still in the process of cleaning him up and putting the finishing touches on Nicki. I am overcome with emotion and puffy-chest pride!

Allen walks me back out to the waiting room and whispers in my ear "I can feel Dad. He is here Mom". Oh fuck if this doesn't open the flood gates. It's a good thing Allen doesn't stick around, because he would see me lose it. I have mixed up emotions; Tears of joy and tears of ache, because Tim should be here for this. Suck it up and tough it out, Molly. There are going to be many monumental moments for Allen and Henry that Tim should have seen. There is nothing I can do or say that will change that their dad can be here in spirit only. I have no doubt that Tim has a front row seat to watch over our sons. I find big comfort in that thought.

Pawpaw Lin is excited to hear the news that the first Grandbaby has made it into the world. If I were a betting woman, I would put down five bucks Lin will be soon shopping for a peddle tractor for Lennon. He reminds me that I have an appointment to show the house in an hour. Shit! I forgot all about it. I have to go home to unlock the house and get the dog. Actually, this works out pretty good since the waiting room is filling up with Nicki's family. I know everyone is doing fine. I will have to wait for my one-on-one G'ma snuggle time. That's ok, sometimes anticipation is a good thing. It just makes the ripe berry taste even sweeter.

Talk about looking at every nook and cranny of a house. These house hunters take two hours to walk through our home. The third time I drive by, they are outside walking around, pointing out the property lines. It looks like they have three boys. That is great since we live two and a half blocks from the school. This has been a perfect house for raising kids. Henry seems ok with selling the house. I know he will miss it, but he also knows his journey is just beginning. Funny thing about my boys, Henry has the logic and Allen the compassion. Case and point: if a bum were walking down the street with no clothes on, Allen would strip naked to give up what he had. Henry would hand him a few dollars and give him a ride to the nearest Goodwill parking lot.

When I finally get home, it is too late for me to go back to the hospital. Allen just called to let me know they are settled in for the night and Lennon is sleeping soundly. The nurses are watching over him while the kids have a nice dinner provided by the hospital.

The next couple of weeks consist of more packing and purging. Lin gets a short break between jobs. The South Bend job didn't pan out, so he took a week off to get the garage cleaned out. It takes every drop of the week to complete this task. Talk about having a lot of shit in one room; the man has three completed Harley's, one up on the rack, and enough parts to build at least two more. Our storage unit is filled to the brim by the time he finishes. The furniture that is left in the house will be sold or given away, because there is no way we can fit one more piece in the storage unit.

Have you ever had an abrupt whirlwind moment in your life (excluding birth and death) that made you step back and say "Oh Fuck, here it comes! See you on the other side?" Selling my house of over 20 years in just two weeks is one of those moments. Lin was back in Texas when I got the call. The new owners wanted immediate possession since they had reached the end of their time limit, part of the deal they made with the people who bought their house. I had three days to empty the rest of the house and find somewhere to live for a couple of days.

So, now I am sitting in a hotel room, wondering what the fuck just happened. As I wait for the final papers to be drawn up, I have mixed emotions. Part of me will miss the memories in that house and another part of me is ready for a new "outside the box" adventure. It helps to know that a loving and growing family will make memories in "my" house. I plan to get this done and join Lin. Come on, Molly, kick down some walls!

I am spending as much time with Lennon as I can without being a pain in the ass. Nicki and Allen are very good parents and they have not yet reached the point of leaving him for any length of time. That's ok, I will respect that. They could be the kind of parents who want to go out and party every weekend while the Grandparents babysit. We talked to the college and they will allow Henry to move into his dorm room a few weeks early. Since summer classes were going on, the powers that be didn't think it would create a problem. So all of our chicks are doing their own thing. For the first time in more years than I care to count, I am the only one under this roof, even if it is a hotel room.

I want to pick a subject in history and learn as much as I can, so I can write a book about it. A point in time that has always interested me, just this side of an obsession is the British Monarchy. I don't know why, but the history of different dynasties holds a strange fascination for me. I have read countless books on the subject. I have not read much about the time before the Tudor dynasty, but from that point forward it is a much studied subject.

Once again, I am struck with the sheer fucking greatness of being able to learn with my own eyes. It is one thing to read a book and another entirely to have all five of your senses involved. I can't be heard by others when I speak. My only concern is the language barrier. Yes, I know that English was spoken in England, but have you ever tried to *read* Shakespeare? I guess as long as I understand the general context, I will have some idea of what is happening. I want to travel back to observe how different eras and countries tie back to one another through family.

I want to get a small taste of this right now, while I am in this quite hotel room all by myself. I have the door locked and no plans for a couple of hours. I want me some realm of

Chapter Twenty-two

Victoria.

Once I let my eyes adjust, because I have evidently decided to come back in the dark again. It figures. I don't mean just a little dark, I mean the only light is *a* candle. I hear people talking in the distance and by the tones of the voices, I don't think I am in any danger. I hear people laughing. That is always a good sign.

My past test (with Dmitri and the pen) tells me that if I pick up said candle, it becomes invisible, right? What happens to the light it projects? If anyone saw this would they see a glowing orb just walking across the room? Sing it with me, in Twilight Zone fashion, "de de de de." Oh sure I could stand perfectly still if someone came into the room, but I would have to blow out the candle and we would both be screwed in the dark. I need to start a list of questions for Dmitri. I may have to use the buddy system with this experiment.

While I have been busy thinking about illuminating my situation, a team of people have come into the room to turn on the lights, I hope. It sounds like they are setting up ladders so I am going to assume there is a chandelier above my head. I am slow to get used to their accents. They don't sound like my daughter-in-law when she talks. It is more guttural and really fucking fast. The couple of words I do make out let me know that they are, in fact, here to show me what I need to see. So, let there be light!

I notice there are four big gold chandeliers above my head. After some discussion, they decide to light all of the candles because of something about "the carriage" and "within the hour". By the way they are dressed, I guess they are servants. There are two men busy on the ladders, two girls handing them new candles, and two younger girls catching the old tapers in the aprons they are wearing. I watch this process with complete fascination. I am picking up that they think something big is going to happen today since they have all been told to wear their black mourning livery. The men are dressed in black suits with tails and two of the ladies; the hand-off girls, are wearing very proper black dresses with small white aprons. The full skirts go to the floor and every button is done up tightly. How do these girls breathe? They have got to be wearing corsets to have a waist that small, not something I would wear to clean the house. The catchers are dressed in simple, fuller black cotton dresses, covered with full length white aprons. The hats they wear look like the sleeping caps the Ingalls sisters wore, only black. (Oh admit it. You watched Little House on the Prairie.) All of them are wearing black bands around their arms. They appear to be awful chipper to be in mourning. They are having fun, turning their task into a game. The younger girls are moving around with their aprons wide open to catch the next toss. The other two ladies giggle into their hands like they aren't allowed to bust out laughing. Shit, for all I know. If they do laugh out loud, they might pop a stitch-or worse-crack a rib.

WOW! WOW! WOW! I look up to see the most magnificent ceiling I have ever had the privilege to see. It is a slightly domed ceiling, painted to look as if it were deeper than it actually is. The colors are gold and a bright robin egg blue. There are rows of gold octagon shapes filled with blue that lead to a larger, open octagon in the middle. If I am not mistaken, the "order of the garter" star is in the center. It is so hard to describe the beauty of what I see. The colors are more brilliant then I have ever imagined. The walls are covered in gold guild and white marble. There are six niches cut into the marble and each has a golden statue based on Greek mythology. There are many golden statue busts placed on shelves, also cut into the marble. You gotta be pretty important to have a gold head. There are windows behind me and straight ahead is a fabulous fireplace and doorways through the other two walls. In the middle of the room, right under the chandeliers, is a very pretty, tall wooden thing sitting on a platform of steps. It reminds me of an oversized pawn piece on a chess board. What is this thing that has a room built around it? I climb over a small railing to get a closer look. After some investigation, I discover this pawn thing is a clock. According to this rather odd clock, it is 5:10 (I assume A.M.). I am not even sure where I am, or a better question, "when" I am. I need to see something or someone I recognize.

The two doorways on each side of the room are a force of their own. Both are made of huge slabs of pillared white marble. Which way do I go? Which way do I go? I follow my new-found friends and exit stage right. Now I am getting discouraged. It is very dark in the room we enter. The only light comes from the room we just walked out of and the two candles the "cinch sisters" are carrying. These people walk like they are late for their own funeral. I catch a glimpse of three windows, but not much light coming in from the outside just yet. I cop a squat on one of the upholstered benches and wait it out. I have a feeling this is too good to miss. What is the point of lighting the other room, but leaving this one in the dark?

As I sit, in dark, I occasionally hear voices, but I can't make out what they are saying. I patiently sit for twenty minutes or so, just day dreaming about where I am. Here comes more footsteps. More than one person is moving around close to me. All I can hear is their feet hitting the floor. All at once all three windows have their shutters opened. This is better than a remote control! There is a chick at each window and these girls have got this down to "synchronized opening". Damn! It is a good thing the light outside is still on the gentle side.

Holy fucking wall of oil paintings, Batman! The main feature here is dark wood paneling. There are paintings of every shape and size on the walls. Finally, there is enough light for me to look at each one. I do not recognize any of these figures. The eras represented blow my mind. Over here I see a rather portly dude in a white wig, and over there I see a beautiful woman with two children, but no powdered wig. Once again, the ceiling is the best. It is covered with a gold guild carving made to look like a very ornate picture frame. The exception is the oval painting in the middle. It is an old painting of a very pretty woman, a man, a cherub, and an angel. The chubby little cherub has wings. The man is dressed in what looks like a soldier uniform. The woman is leaning on what I think is his shield. The plaster surrounding the painting is immense. An earthquake, standing right here, would kill me!

Something I haven't given much thought to: Can I take pictures? There are not sufficient words in the dictionary to convey the beauty of what I have seen in these two rooms. It would bring up a whole new question back home: What if the room I am standing in doesn't exist anymore? Where did Miss Molly Nobody get digital pictures of a place that was, let's say, demolished in World War 1? It would be incredible to have something to reference while I write my book. The downside though is it would create more secrets. I would have to keep a box under lock and key, in a trunk buried in an attic full of memory cards. This will take some more thought and planning.

I look out the windows and see a large courtyard surrounded by three stories of brick. There are many doors and windows. The building I am in is just one of several. This place is huge! This has got to be a palace, but which one? I can tell by the grandeur and the uptight faces in the paintings that this is Royalty. I don't think just anyone can have a star representing the "order of the garter". Am I in the Hanover dynasty?

The three ladies who opened the windows have decided to huddle and giggle amongst themselves. I get closer and hope they will say something to help me figure out where I am. I must have caught these girls on a good day. My nose is not being offended. The red-haired girl is doing most of the talking.

"Sad lot that one; Maybe the fat slob can sleep wif his dead giraffe," she says. They all giggle in unison.

What in the hell does that mean? I don't get the joke.

The taller girl responds, "We are the better for it. You wait and see. Bernie from the stables tells me the Duchess is meeting up wif the Sir this morning. They have sent the coach for him."

Red pipes up again, "I hope we make it seven more years or that wretched woman will be in charge." The quiet one says something, but the only two words I get are "pet" and "Conroy". Once again there is a big round of giggles. The girls snap to attention when a man marches in and huffs out "The carriage has arrived". All three scurry off like rabbits. Big Huffy man walks, almost marches towards the clock room. I have no choice but to follow.

As I walk back into the grand room, I see a few people quietly exit through the door straight across from me. Damn, these people are quiet! I didn't even know there was anyone in here, but me and stuffy pants. The candles are still smoking from being snuffed. The window shutters are now open. Things don't stay quiet for long; I hear footsteps heading our way, coming from the same direction everyone just scurried towards. In other words, stage left.

A group of four people enter the room. The Lady who erupts into the room large and in charge is obviously a Royal. There are two girls buzzing around her, picking at her clothes like there is a thread out of place. Miss Thing has had enough of being picked at and brushes the girls away with one upward sweep of her hand. No words are necessary. Mr. Huffy bows his head and says "Sir Conroy will be here momentarily Ma'am". I did hear the quiet girl correctly earlier, she did say "Conroy". Now I know when I am. The grand Lady in front of me is the Duchess of Kent, Queen Victoria's mother. She is a very pretty woman, with her dark hair all done up on her head, in big curls. She is not wearing a hat but she has a very pretty headband mixed in with the curls. The earrings and broach she wears are made of black stones, not much on bling-bling. I can tell she is very excited about something, in a good way, I think. She appears to be very pleased with herself and smug. Her eyes are lit up and she is having a hard time retaining her composure. For someone dressed in mourning clothes to have this much excitement running through them, it can't be good. I smell a plot, and too much perfume. Damn, too much of a good thing is fugly!

Here comes the other up-to-no-good half of the equation. Sir Conroy struts into the room like a cocky rooster on parade. Get a load of him! Once our fair Duchess sees him, all bets are off. She quickly glides across the room and puts her hand out for him to take in his. Oh, what a suck-up! He bows, kissing her hand and says "My dearest Lady".

Ok little back story here. From what I have already learned from history. The Duchess and Conroy are out to get whatever they can from Princess Victoria. They both know she is their life-long meal ticket. They are convinced that Victoria will take the throne before she turns 18, the legal age. This means she will need a regent to do her bidding. Who better than her mother? This poor woman who loves her daughter, will attempt to do the right thing. At the end of the day it will be Conroy pushing all of her buttons. They are both greedy and manipulative. If they keep the young girl under their control, she won't be able to think for herself and will come to them for guidance, not. As history will show, the "Kensington" system will blow up in their faces.

The Duchess lets Conroy know she has asked him to meet her here because she has some work to do, now that Victoria is "heir presumptive". She takes him by the arm and leads him "stage left". Of course, I follow.

Another "Wow" room; the walls are covered in a crimson velvet wallpaper. This gives a whole new meaning to the fuzzy "black light" posters I had as a kid. The two paintings in this room are enormous. They are scenic. Everything is framed in over-the-top gold. There are a few chairs and benches along the walls around the room. Straight ahead are three large windows. The Duchess marches towards the windows, then makes an immediate left through the door beside a wonderful fireplace.

Compared to all of the other rooms, this one is pretty plain and simple. This room has not one hint of being lived in. It smells like it has been recently cleaned. It's not Lysol I smell, it's more like a diluted vinegar. Would it make sense if I said this room is a shell with no life? The walls are covered with massive pieces of heavy paneling. There are a couple of tapestries hanging from the wall, and a few paintings. I notice one of the smaller pieces must have been a replacement because, there is a change in the color of the wood behind it. I also noticed that the art of hanging a picture on a nail must not apply to Royalty. All of the paintings are hanging from cords connected to the crown molding or ceiling. I guess that makes sense, since castles and palaces aren't constructed with drywall…yet.

The Duchess has pulled a cord, and from the instant rush of servants who enter the forum, I think it is safe to say it is a servant's bell. Lord have mercy! This woman starts barking out orders to remove the furniture, what little there is. It is obvious to everyone, the bitch is back and she is taking over. She is harder to understand than the servant girls were earlier, with a heavy German accent. Good old "Con" is just standing there, watching her, with a shit-eating grin on his face. When he does speak up, he simply says "This will cause quite a stir". Before God gets that news, the room is void of a bed. This was not an easy job, since it was the largest piece of furniture in the room. They take it apart and carry it out in pieces.

I peek into the crimson room and a small audience has gathered. I hear one of them say "Mind yourself, she's at it again. The five do it all girls have been cleaning the King's rooms for days, leaving us a few people down. Even took paintings out of packing. Now I know why." There are the "cinch sisters" and the "shutter slappers". I wonder how many servants are employed here.

The Duchess has gone bat-shit crazy! Now, she is spinning circles in the middle of the room, with her arms up in the air as she manages to hold on to her shoulder shawl. It almost looks like she has wings coming out of the side of her head. When she stops going in circles, she grabs "Con" and says "Now is my time, come wit me! We have a list of demands to make, starting wit Dowager Princess of Wales, and I owe no one". Back through the door way we go, and she doesn't seem to notice the small crowd of parting servants. They all shit n' git to move out of her way. The race is on! We go back through the room with the big clock.

Now, we enter a room that I haven't seen yet. It doesn't look like I am going to see it now, either, if I want to keep up with her. I am missing all of the good shit. What the hell? You know the feeling you get when something stops you cold in your tracks? The one where your feet stop on a dime and your mouth falls open in amazement. I am there.

In front of me is the most amazing staircase I have ever seen! I don't want to know what "Crazy Lady" is up to now. There are three tiers of black stairs and each one has a landing comprised of black and white tiles in the checkerboard pattern. There is a marvelous wrought iron railing going all of the way down, or up, depending on which way you are going. The walls are covered with a mural of people. Yes, people. They are all wearing clothes from a past century. They are leaning over a painted baluster, like they are watching a parade walk down the steps. A couple of the ladies look to be passing secrets, or flirting with the handsome man beside them. The entire wall is painted to make up this scene, complete with beautiful, deep, and dimensional archways. The gallery of spectators look as if they are standing on a balcony overlooking the stair case. There are three arches painted on the larger wall that runs parallel with the stairs.

The first archway on the long wall depicts two guys that look like English Yeoman in puffy-sleeved red uniforms. They are holding spears. A young boy is standing on this side of the baluster, with a very sheepish grin on his face. There are five full human forms along with pieces and parts of others in the background. Depicted in the second is a young lady leaning over (let it all hang out sister), flirting with a man that looks like Christopher Columbus. Beside him is a cute little blonde girl wearing a blue bonnet, holding an adorable puppy. There are seven full human faces and a forehead with eyes in the background (ain't got nobody, nobody got me ala Marty Feldman) trying to peek over the people "down in front". The last arch has two guys wearing turbans. One looks almost like Santa Claus, out of uniform, and the other is a man of color wearing a brilliant blue sash and sitting on the railing with one leg hanging over the edge. An uninterested young lady is looking beyond a guy who appears to be trying to pick her up. Sorry Dude, the pink uniform and blue cape was your first mistake. There are six full faces I see here.

   The smaller wall at the top of the second flight features one arch. Damn, there is a man that looks like the dude on the oatmeal box holding a cane, you know, the "Quaker guy." The lady beside him is pulling a "King of Pop" baby-over-the-railing move. The little boy between them has some strange-looking eyes, almost wild. There is another hoochey momma leaning over the rail, holding a really ugly white dog. There are six figures depicted, plus a side view of an old man turning away. The detail is incredible! I am in awe of how realistic the whole scene is.

The Royals sure do have a thing for gorgeous ceilings. This one is really hard to describe. The outer perimeter of the design is a broken, golden square, like four perfect corners with flawless separate squares in the middle, and an interrupted line on each side. A big textbook square in the middle holding a fat golden circle. Inside the circle is a large curved "X". Each quadrant features different faces. One exhibits three ministerial men. Another, a stocky man holding a painters pallet. I wish I could get closer to see the details. I count thirteen figures gazing down at me. Inside the "X" is a smaller centered circle with a long rod that has what I assume is a light hanging at the end of it, like the pendulum on a grandfather clock.

I take a seat at the bottom of the second tier of steps. I need to write some of this shit down, and the sunlight coming in beats the hell out of being in the dark. My brain is reaching overload, to the point of a mental shutdown, the crash after the rush. I have managed to write down one-word reminders and doodled a couple of pictures. If I do some research when I get back, I should be able to pinpoint this castle. If this is what I am going to write about, then I need to suck it all in slowly. I know me, if I get too much information then I will leave out some of the really fucking cool details. It makes me think of an old joke. Two bulls are standing on a hill, looking at a herd of cows below them. The young bull says," Let's run down there and fuck a couple cows". The old bull says, "Let's walk and fuck them all".

My original plan was to take a trip to see Victoria on the day in 1830 that she became next in line for the throne, after King George IV passed away. Good job on landing! I got the day correct. The Duchess confirmed it when she mentioned Victoria "now heir presumptive". I haven't done a very good job though, of "seeing" the purpose of this trip. I don't hear anyone, so it is hard to tell where I need to go next. Do I just sit here and wait for someone to walk by, or do I explore on my own?

I like seeing people when I travel. The scenery plays a key part in the lure. I want to do this for a living. The people, the way they live in their environments, the scenery is intoxicating. The little boy looking for his Dad's name on the dead soldier list, flashes into my mind. I want to go home and do some research so I can take this one step at a time. I will do this the right way, not fast and stupid.

"Maybe someday we will find that it wasn't really

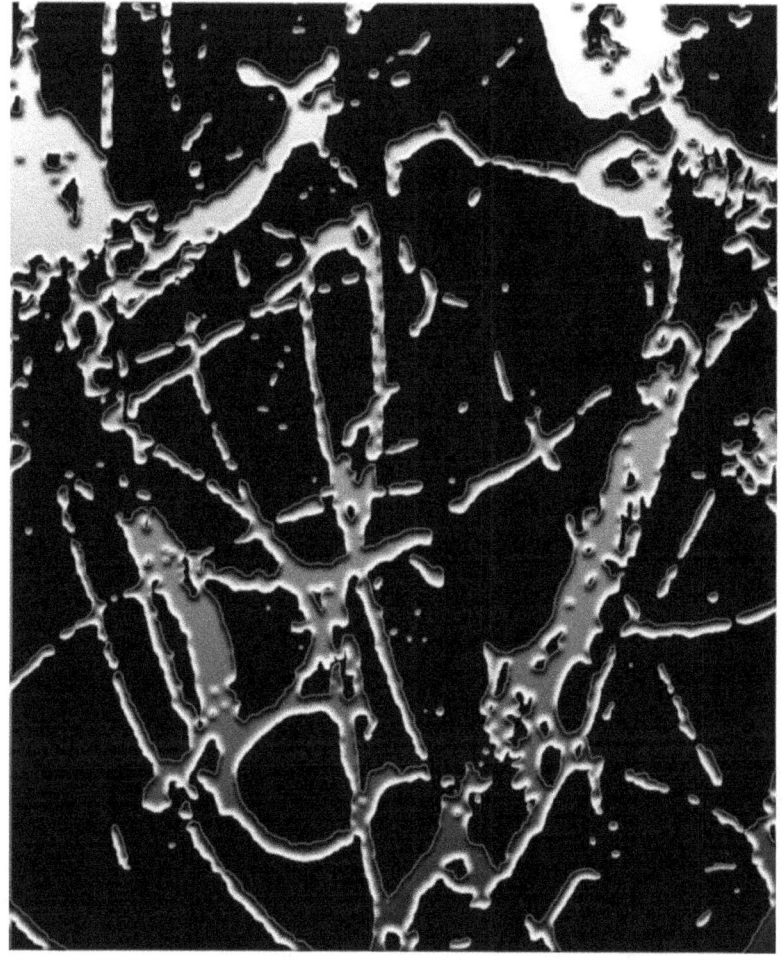

Chapter Twenty-three

Wasted time…"

Nothing like coming back to Don Henley in my brain, I like it!

I spend the remainder of the afternoon looking up everything I saw. I determine that I visited Kensington Palace. Princess Victoria was, in fact, there. The Duchess and Conroy took her on tours of England not long after she became the next in line. King William IV took offense to the tours. He did not like the Duchess and detested Conroy. He made the following speech at his birthday party in August 1836. It says it all.

"I trust in God that my life may be spared for nine months longer, after which period, in the event of my death, no regency would take place. I should then have the satisfaction of leaving the royal authority to the personal exercise of that young lady, the heiress presumptive of the crown, and not in the hands of a person now near me who is surrounded by evil advisors".

Now that all of the paperwork has been signed, sealed and delivered. I am free to join Lin. All things and loved ones are taken care of in Indiana. I am sitting in another hotel room in Memphis. This is about the half-way point of a long drive. I am working on a list of trips I want to take. I also have an ever-growing list of questions I want answered. I have positively decided that I want to wonder through the different reigns of the English Monarchy. This is what I want to write my book about. This will be my niche.

I have given much thought to the question of taking a camera with me. The notion of letting someone else develop the pictures is out of the question. The only option is a secret digital camera that I will have to keep hidden. Then, I will have to destroy the memory card once I am done with the information. This sounds like a lot of work, and considering we will be living in a camper, a pain in the ass. As of now, I am going to stick with good old pen and paper. If Lin reads my scribbles I can tell him they are just notes from my research. That wouldn't be a lie, or a secret. I am skating on thin ice with my conscience the way it is already, without adding more to it. I like sleep way too much to have it interrupted by guilt. I know the way my mind works, good, bad or indifferent.

When I finally reach Lin, we spend the first few days getting settled into our new way of life together. I am here to tell you. It doesn't suck! It takes me a couple of days to realize I am not on vacation. I have nothing to do but take care of the here and now. Lin seems to enjoy being taken care of; no more eating on the go, worrying about laundry, or cleaning up after himself. My man gets pampered after a long day.

Lin just left for work and I am going back to Kensington. The beauty of this trip is that I have all day. We are going to The Wharf tonight for seafood. Unlike our house, the camper takes an hour to clean, stem to stern.

Lin's co-worker, Mark owns a large amount of property and has allowed us to park our camper in a remote corner among the trees. Since we are self-sufficient, with a generator, this is very do-able. The only parts that suck are when the shit tank has to be emptied, or the water tanks need filled. I have mastered the art of pissing outside. That's not a bad tradeoff for the seclusion and beauty of the current scenery.

All systems are go! I want to see Victoria before….

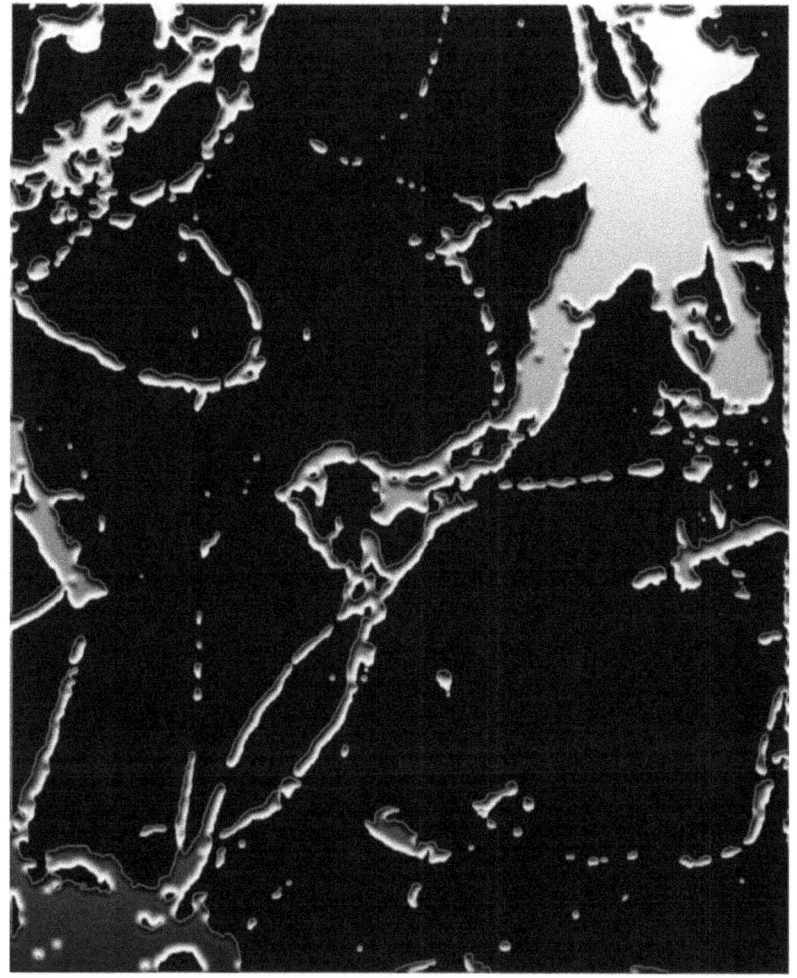

www.ingramcontent.com/pod-product-compliance
Lightning Source LLC
Chambersburg PA
CBHW071214090426
42736CB00014B/2814